# THE TOMB OF AMENEMHAB

## No.44 AT QURNAH

HASSAN EL-SAADY

OXBOW | books
Oxford & Philadelphia

*To Professor K.A. Kitchen*
*Who paved my way in Egyptology*
*with gratitude, affection and appreciation*

This edition published in the United Kingdom in 2024 by
OXBOW BOOKS
81 St Clements, Oxford OX4 1AW

and in the United States by
OXBOW BOOKS
1950 Lawrence Road, Havertown, PA 19083



Paperback Edition: ISBN 979-8-88857-085-2
Digital Edition: ISBN 979-8-88857-086-9 (epub)

First published in 1996 by Aris & Phillips Ltd

Oxbow Books is grateful to the Petrie Museum for their collaboration in bringing out these new editions



Printed in the United Kingdom by CMP Digital Print Solutions

For a complete list of Oxbow titles, please contact:

UNITED KINGDOM
Oxbow Books
Telephone (0)1226 734350
Email: oxbow@oxbowbooks.com
www.oxbowbooks.com

UNITED STATES OF AMERICA
Oxbow Books
Telephone (610) 853-9131, Fax (610) 853-9146
Email: queries@casemateacademic.com
www.casemateacademic.com/oxbow

Oxbow Books is part of the Casemate Group

*Front cover:* The Tomb of Amenemhab: chapel, south wall, niche (image: Eva Hofmann, Egyptological Institute Heidelberg, © Heidelberg University Library, free access)

# Contents

## List of Plates

# Abbreviations

| | |
|---|---|
| ***AE*** | Ancient Egypt, London, New York. |
| ***ASAE*** | Annales du service des antiquités de l'Egypte, Le Caire. |
| ***BIFAO*** | Bullctin de l'institut français d'archéologie orientale, Le Caire. |
| ***Bonnet, Reallex.*** | H. Bonnet, Reallexikon der ägyptischen Religionsgeschichte, Berlin 1953. |
| ***Faulkner, CD*** | R. O. Faulkner, A Concise Dictionary of Middle Egyptian, Oxford 1962 |
| ***JEA*** | Journal of Egyptian Archaeology, London. |
| ***KRI*** | K. A. Kitchen, Ramesside Inscriptions, 8 vols., Oxford 1968-90. |
| ***LA*** | Lexikon der Ägyptologie, Wiesbaden. |
| ***MDAIK*** | Mitteilungen des Deutschen Archäologischen Instituts, Kairo. |
| ***Mond's MSS*** | Sir Robert Mond Manuscripts (unpublished), University of Liverpool, Dept. of Archaeology. |
| ***Or*** | Orientalia, Nova Series, Rome. |
| ***PM*** | B. Porter, R. Moss, Topographical Bibliography of Ancient Egyptian Hieroglyphic Texts, Reliefs and Paintings, 7 vols, Oxford, 2 ed. 1966 ff. |
| ***Ranke, PN*** | H. Ranke, Die altägyptischen Personennamen, 2 Bde, Glückstadt 1935 u. 1952. |
| ***Rec Trav*** | Recueil de travaux relatifs à la philologie et l'archéologie égyptiennes et assyriennes, Paris. |
| ***Urk.*** | Urkunden des aegyptischen Altertums, begr. von G. Steindorff. |
| ***Wb*** | Wörterbuch der ägyptischen Sprache, hg. von A. Erman und H. Grapow, 6 Bde, Berlin u. Leipzig$^{2}$ 1957. |
| ***ZÄS*** | Zeitschrift für Ägyptische Sprache und Altertumskunde, Leipzig, Berlin. |

# Preface

In his catalogue of private tombs, Sir Alan Gardiner described the effort of Sir Robert Mond in this field 90 years ago by these words: "The scheme of conservation set on foot by Mr. Mond ought to ensure the permanence of the Private Tombs for many generations to come".

In fact, the present writer never dreamt to be one of those coming generations until Prof. K. A. Kitchen generously entrusted me with fulfilling part of the task, by publishing T.44. He also kindly sponsored my nomination by the Griffith Institute to hold a Gardiner Trust Scholarship in 1992 for this project.

This work has been carried on since 1992, with many delays due to my academic duties mainly in the Faculty of Arts of the University of Alexandria besides other universities on delegation. I paid two long visits to England and another four to Luxor which enabled me positively to concentrate and complete the work in its final form.

I would like to thank, in the very beginning, Prof. Kitchen also for his loyal help and friendship not only during this advanced work but since I worked under his supervision as a Ph. D. student in 1986. For this work, he kindly supplied me with most of the initial copies of the tomb inscriptions and many photographs which presented its solid base, as well as reading the first draft of this book.

I have pleasure also in expressing my thanks to the Griffith Institute, represented by Dr. Helen Whitehouse, where the Gardiner Scholarship enabled me to tackle this work with confidence and keenness.

My thanks go further to Prof. Mohammed Abdul-Halim Nour El-Dine, General Co-ordinator of the Supreme Council of Antiquities in Egypt, whose official permission to publish this tomb and to work on the site for many times, made my visits to Luxor so useful.

I am also grateful to Prof. Omar Abdul-Aziz Omar, the ex-dean of the Faculty of Arts at Alexandria and the present Deputy Chairman of the University of Alexandria, for his encouragement and understanding which facilitated my visit to Liverpool to start the scholarship during the relevant academic year.

My thanks also go to my colleagues both in the Department of History and Archaeology at Alexandria who had taken on the burden of my courses during my absence, and in the School of Archaeology at Liverpool for their kind assistance.

Additionally, I would like to thank Dr. J. Malek and Ms. A. Dexter, for supplying me with Schott photographs; and to Mr. Zaghloul Ibrahim, chief inspector at Giza, for drawing the linear plates of this book; also to Mr. Mohammed Abd-Allah and Mr. Ashraf Okasha, chief inspectors in the Qurna inspectorate of Antiquities, for useful assistance in my visits to the site.

I am so thankful to the publishers "Aris & Phillips", for their interest and kindness in accepting this book.

Finally, to my wife Sofia and my two daughters Esraa and Alaa, I owe sincere and warm gratitude for their patience and supportiveness.

Hassan M. El-Saady
Alexandria- Egypt.
1417 H.- 1996.

## Foreword

It is a pleasure for me here to introduce this publication of a largely overlooked monument in the great necropolis of Western Thebes, produced by one of Egypt"s rising younger scholars under all the usual pressures that beset academics worldwide, in terms of teaching, supervision, administration, limited resources, etc., which inhibit opportunities and flow of research and publication for so many of us.

Recording and publication of Egypt's standing monuments is an ever more urgent desideratum. Changing climatic and hydrological factors and the ever-present threat of human interference (robbing of decoration, as in this tomb) alike conspire to make such a task an absolute priority, if invaluable primary sources for studying Ancient Egypt are to be saved for study, both for future generations and for ourselves. Such work is increasingly taking on the flavour of an ongoing 'rescue operation' in the conditions of today.

Therefore, this present volume is a welcome addition to this urgent enterprise. Tomb 44, it must be said, is a deceptive charmer! At first sight, it offers an attractive series of brightly-painted wall-scenes to the visitor. But a closer inspection reveals a more sober reality. The painted surfaces of the scenes are widely marred by frequent smaller bare patches, while in some scenes large areas of decoration are broken away entirely. And to a very large extent, the rapidly-painted black hieroglyphs of the texts have largely faded or worn away, often leaving only uneven and tantalising traces, very many of which are now beyond the point of convincing decipherment even on the original walls (let alone on photos).

Such intractable problems have required practical solutions. Thus, the major part of the decoration of this tomb-chapel is now made available in a combination of basic line-drawings and photographs, which show the present state of the monument. The fruits of concentrated work on the inscriptions by Dr. El-Saady and this writer at various intervals (separately and together) have been brought together in the series of text-figures that precede the plates proper. By these means, with the limited resources available, a practical record of Tomb 44 can now be made available to all.

Dr. El-Saady has taken our knowledge about the priest Amenemhab and his family further than previously; he has been able to show that Amenemhab and his tomb belong almost certainly within the reign of the ubiquitous Ramesses II, and can offer a possible link with another Theban tomb. So this work shows gains in knowledge, as well as presenting a little-known monument.

Woolton, Liverpool, 14th August, 1996 K.A. Kitchen.

# Introduction

At Sheikh-Abd-el-Qurnah cemetery, some distance south east of the group of tombs nos. 41- 42 and 110, just east of no. 113 lies the tomb no. 44 of Amenemhab.[1] It belongs in general to the series of undated private tombs in the Theban necropolis, and to that of the Ramesside era in particular. Except for its mention in ***PM*** [2], neither a comprehensive single publication exists nor any major mention in the outstanding and essential references for such studies.[3]

Thus, it seemed very stimulating to the present writer to accept the challenge of the hard task of publishing T.44. Apart from its small size, the difficulty seems technically to be the lost and mutilated parts of the tomb which would need considerable comparative investigations to restore in full. Yet another problem is the specific dating of the tomb, although it has been already classified amongst the Ramesside private tombs. A fact which is apparent from observing the Ramesside style with few exceptions. The design consists of a rock-cut chapel and most likely an underground chamber (yet undiscovered). The superstructure has the broad hall (*wsḫt*) which functions significantly as a hall of audience or reception room and the long hall which runs axially deep within the rock ending with a niche, as in our example; and it corresponds with the private rooms in houses.

The paintings according to the Ramesside style are rich in colours, floral borders and specific designs (stars, squares, lozenges). In earlier times, tomb-scenes followed the pattern of worldly themes dominating the broad hall, whilst those of religious tone dominated the long hall. Such a distribution is represented only in a very restricted scale in T.44.

These scenes are of debased style compared with the private tombs of the early New Kingdom, partly because of the unsmooth surface of mixture of mud and coarse straw as well as the unsystematic composition of mural themes with their profuse details on a dull yellow ground.[4] Here also, that the prevailing offering formulae *rdit, i3w n* or *n k3.n di.n* are those found in most of the Ramesside tombs, instead of the ordinary formulae of *ḥtp di nsw* or *irt ḥtp di nsw*.[5]

Moreover, there is a lack of historical scenes, as the owner and his family ar merely potential ministrants. This latter fact is very prominent in T.44, and adds to thi study the major problem of trying to designate the reign of the Ramesside king unde whom the tomb's owner, Amenemhab, lived and served Amon in Thebes.

The plan of this present study is arranged in four chapters, and an introductio which throws light on the general features of the Ramesside private tombs as found i T.44. Also it demonstrates the problems and obstacles of the study which the presen writer encountered.

The first chapter first gives the setting of T.44 among the cemetery of Sheikh Abd-el-Qurnah in particular and the Theban necropolis in general. Secondly, thi chapter deals with the architectural features and the scheme of decoration in this tomb.

The second chapter deals with the broad hall of the tomb as well as its entranc and ceiling, by describing the remaining scenes and translating their inscriptions.

The third chapter presents the scenes and texts of the long hall and its niche The fourth chapter seeks to throw light on the owner of the tomb: his career an family.

The study ends with conclusions, drawing several points from discussin specific matters in the main part of the book.

I would also mention that the two asterisks (**) found many times in this study refer to the texts which were transcribed by the present writer on the site and were no found in the transcriptions of Sir R. Mond and Prof. K. A. Kitchen. On plates B H refers to the Broad Hall, and L H to the Long Hall.

## Notes

[1] A. Gardiner & A. Weigall, *A Topographical Catalogue of the Private Tombs of Thebes*, London, 1913, pl. VII c2.

[2] ***PM***$^2$ I/I, 84-5.

[3] Such as Hay ***MSS***; or J. F. Champollion, *Monuments de L'Egypte et de la Nubie, Notices Descriptives,* 2 vols., Paris, 1844-79; or R. Lepsius, *Denkmäler aus Aegypten und Aethiopien,* 12 vols., Berlin, 1849- 59, *Text,* 5 vols., 1897- 1913; W. Wreszinski, *Atlas zur Altaegyptischen Kulturgeschichte,* Leipzig, 1923- 35.

[4] A. Badawy, *A History of Egyptian Architecture*, vol. III, Berkely, 1968, 408- 10, & N. de G. Davies, *Two Ramesside Tombs at Thebes*, New York, 1927, XVIII.

[5] M. Abdul-Qader, *The Development of the Funerary Beliefs and Practices Displayed in the Private Tombs of the New Kingdom at Thebes*, Cairo, 1966, 195.

## Preface to the 2024 edition

In the 1970s, a much-anticipated new series of publications illustrated objects and themes related to the excavations of the archaeologist William Matthew Flinders Petrie (1853–1942) in Egypt, and aspects of the collection of University College London's Petrie Museum of Egyptian and Sudanese Archaeology. A young couple setting up in business in the early 1970s, Aris and Phillips published these works, written by members of the UCL Egyptology Department, in their *Modern Egyptology* series. Building on Petrie's own observations, the authors of these volumes aimed to complete the great task of publishing the Petrie Museum of Egyptian and Sudanese Archaeology's vast collection, and to present some of the research that Petrie himself was not able to address in his own published works during his lifetime. As the current Curator of the Petrie Museum, it is a great privilege for me to support Oxbow Books in their mission to republish the series, which remains a key source of information for all those interested in object-based approaches to the study of the ancient world.

The Petrie Museum, part of University College London (UCL), is home to one of the largest and most significant collections of Egyptian and Sudanese archaeology in the world. Free to visit, this extraordinary collection tells stories about the lives of ordinary people who lived along the Nile Valley thousands of years ago. Originally set up as a teaching collection, the Petrie Museum comprises over 80,000 objects housed together with an internationally important archaeological archive. It is a collection of world firsts and 'oldests': the oldest woven garment; the oldest worked iron objects; the first known depiction of loom weaving; the oldest known written document about women's health; the earliest veterinary treatise; the oldest will on paper. The Museum has Designated Status from Arts Council England, meaning that it is considered to have outstanding resonance and national cultural significance. The collection has a substantial, visible international reputation for research, supporting hundreds of researchers every year, both remotely and in person.

The Petrie Museum is named after Flinders Petrie, who was appointed in 1892 as the first Professor of Egyptian Archaeology and Philology in the UK at UCL. Over three-quarters of the material in the Museum comes from excavations directed or funded by Petrie, or from purchases he made for university teaching. In 1880 at the age of 26, Petrie travelled to Egypt to survey the Great Pyramid. For the next five decades he was at the forefront of the development of archaeology in Egypt and later in Palestine, and his detailed methodological approach continues to shape the discipline today.

Petrie worked at more sites, with greater speed, than any modern archaeologist: seeing his life as a mission of rescue archaeology, Petrie aimed to retrieve as much information as possible from sites that were shrinking dramatically in size as Egypt modernised during the late 19th and early 20th centuries. He published a large part, but not all, of the finds from his excavations in his illustrated typological volumes, arranged according to object types and themes. Today, much of the Petrie Museum's collection is displayed and stored in a way which reflects these publications: for example, several storage cupboards are dedicated to the material illustrated in the 'Objects of Daily Use' volume, and objects in the drawers are arranged according to the order of the published plates. This offers a unique opportunity for researchers to engage with Petrie's typological and methodical approach to archaeology, as well as with the history of museum collections.

The first catalogue to be published in the *Modern Egyptology* series was *Amarna: City of Akhenaten and Nefertiti* in 1972 by Julia Samson, Petrie Museum Honorary Research Assistant. As official publishers to the UCL Egyptology Department the series went on to produce facsimile reprints of eight of Flinders Petrie's most important site reports and many of his object catalogues, originally published through the British School of Archaeology in Egypt. The substantial annual royalties from these reprints were paid into the 'Petrie Fund' at the time, which provided special grants to students in financial need.

In many ways, the new reprints of this classic series can be seen as the latest layer in a vast 'publication stratigraphy' of the thousands of finds from Flinders Petrie's excavations, which now live in museum collections around the world. On reading these volumes, I hope that readers will also be inspired to learn more about the Petrie Museum collection and its fascinating history.

Dr Anna Garnett
Petrie Museum of Egyptian and Sudanese Archaeology, University College London
January 2023

## Publisher's preface

Oxbow Books is pleased to present this title in our *Classics in Egyptology* series. This series of facsimile re-issues is comprised of two sub-series. The first consists of 16 typological catalogues produced by W.M. Flinders Petrie based on his massive collection of Egyptian artefacts. Mostly excavated by Petrie during many seasons of campaign in the last years of the 19th and early decades of the 20th century, they now reside in the Petrie Museum at University College London. Published between 1898 and 1937 and long out of print, the catalogues were re-issued in facsimile by publishers Aris and Phillips in the 1970s. These were followed in the next 15 years or so by publication of a number of newly commissioned titles, based on more recent examination of elements of the Petrie Collection by contemporary experts, under the name *Modern Egyptology*. A selection of these additional titles forms the second component of our own series.

The archaeology of Egypt continues to fascinate. Multi-disciplinary investigation and research continues unabated, encompassing methodologies, scientific and data processing techniques, theoretical approaches, and even whole paradigms that were unheard of in the 1970s and undreamt of when Petrie was working in Egypt. Yet all the titles included in this series continue to be invaluable sources of basic data, providing an unparalleled resource that can easily be cross-referenced with the actual materials they describe and discuss. They remain within the Petrie Collection where they may be accessed and re-examined as new research flourishes. As historic documents, the Petrie catalogues stand as exemplars of the craft of typological classification, the backbone of modern archaeology – much of which, though refined by absolute dating and another 100 years of research, still stands the test of time.

### A note on presentation

The facsimile titles of Petrie's catalogues re-issued in the 1970s were produced from scans of the original publications. Scanning technology at that time was not of the standard or resolution of today. The scans are no longer available, nor has it been possible to obtain, and in doing so destroy, original copies of the Petrie catalogues. These titles have therefore, of necessity, been rescanned from the 1970s re-issues. Where necessary the pages have been digitally enhanced for clarity of reading and to ensure the good quality of the plates, though inevitably a few are not of the standard we might wish, because of the quality of the previous scan, and occasional blocks of text are not precisely 'straight' or evenly situated on the page. However, some pages in the 1970s re-issues had been inserted in the wrong order and this has been corrected. The originals were produced at a folio size. The pages have been reduced slightly to standard A4 for ease of shelving and because this has the effect of slightly improving the scanned images. In some cases, illustrations were presented to scale and the original scale is given on the plate. There were also no digital files available for titles included in the *Modern Egyptology* series, so these too have been scanned from printed copies.

# Chapter 1

## The Site and General Description

## 1- The Site and Situation

It is well known amongst scholars that Elwet Sheikh -Abdel Qurnah is one of the most important cemeteries of private tombs in Thebes. It covers a vast area of steep hills west and north west of the Ramesseum and looking northwards to Deir el Bahari. It is mostly occupied by groups of openings going into the rock from the flat surfaces. These eventually represent the so-called house-like chapels and the tombs of high dignitaries, mainly in the Ramesside Period. The main group of tombs is surrounded by two enclosures. The upper one has two gates; the southern gate is in front of tomb 100 and the northern gate is in front of tomb 69. The lower enclosure separates between the north eastern side of the hill of Sheikh-Abdel Qurnah and that of El- Khokhah with an entrance on its south western side.[1]

As for the situation of Tomb 44, the topic of this account, we may locate it out amongst the group of the lower enclosure, just east of tomb 113 and south east of those numbered as 41, 42, 110 as some distance away . Hence it is located in Sheikh Abdel-Qurnah north as so called by Porter& Moss.[2]

The tomb is cut in a perpendicular cliff of limestone and shale (**pl. A1**). Since it is not accessible for tourists,(probably since Mond's first season) the tomb is safeguarded by a locked iron door and a pile of heaped-up stones in the entrance.[3]

## 2 - General Description

### a - The Architectural Features

Most of the tombs were provided with either a private or shared courtyard, now mostly disappeared. They were built in front of the tombs and left open or prepared in the facade of the mountain where three sides are cut in the rock and the fourth is built of mud- brick as a front wall. Few cases show the court hewn completely in the hill, also some had pillars.[4]

As for Tomb 44 we have a very dubious reference in Mond's ***MSS***, since he refers to his finding to another house of a tomb guardian together with roots of a vine and palm which had been planted in the courtyard, without any mention as to which tomb this courtyard belongs. We would suggest according to his report that it belongs to tomb 23, the main find of the season, or to one of the three or four discovered tombs in the area, including Tomb 44.

The plan consisting of a hall, axial passage and shrine with niche seems to be the general scheme of the tomb as been described *infra*, being a so-called inverted T-shaped tomb chapel (**pl. A2**). This general plan tends to be the most common at Thebes with slight differences in size or entrance or pillars or niches etc., since the late 18th. Dynasty up to the Ramesside period.

The axis of the tomb is oriented slightly due north- east to south -west leading from the doorway to the inner niche. The tomb has no side chambers as well as no columns in any of its parts.[5] The length of the axis is *ca.* 9.3 m. and demonstrates the following features :

***I-The doorway*** : It is now secured by an iron gate without any outer or inner particular features. Probably space for a pyramidion above it, as shown on a scene of the tomb,[6] but it is difficult to prove any relevant trace. It is of *ca.* 2 m. height and 1 m. width.

***II- The entrance*** : Its length is 1.30 m.,and of *ca.* 1.80 m. height. The width is *ca.* 1.20 m. The surfaces completely lack scenes owing to their destruction and their replacement by a cement layer instead. It gives access to a broad hall.

***III- The broad hall*** : It extends across the axis from east to west for a length of *ca.* *5.5* m. It is divided into two halves by the entrance of the tomb and that of the long hall southwards. Its width is *ca.* 2.10 m., and the height is *ca.*2.35 m.

***IV- The long hall*** : It starts from an entrance of a height less than that of its ceiling. The entrance is of *ca.* 81 cm. Then the passage (2.10 m.)which leads to the long hall has two thiknesses, the inner one wider than the entrance. The inner thicknesses measures *ca.* 120 cm. width and 182 length. The rear surfaces of the thiknesses form the north side of the long hall and are of *ca.* 41 cm. on each side of the doorway. The length of the hall itself is *ca.* 3.60 m. and the width which is wider than the entrance passage is of *ca.* 2.20 m.

At the center of the southern wall of the long hall a rectangular niche exists, and it is of 65 cm. depth, 58 cm. width and 75 cm. hight.

As for the burial shaft ; it is worth note that the investigation of the floor in the long hall did not give any trace of digging there. Thus it is most likely that the shaft might have been dug in the outer court of the tomb, either on the right or the left of its entrance according to the Ramesside style. Further excavations would reveal this point of research , because no excavations were done around T.44, as far as I know, since the discoveries by Mond in 1905-6. This problematic point left the consideration of the tomb as chapel or a real tomb with burial shaft beyond our reach.

Moreover, the two obscure allusions about the burial pit cannot be discarded. Although both are based on the discovered remains of a tomb , but the first refers to tomb 53 and the second to tomb 23 as T.44. In Sir Robert Mond's *M*SS, the list of objects refers to tomb 53 while the inscriptions of them are labelled as T.44. Also he mentions in his diary that, during his work in tomb 23 to clear away large amounts of debris, in a southerly direction he discovered in the rock three or four tombs. The best preserved is that of Amenemhab T.44. Quoting him further: " Below this tomb I found remains for an entirely unfinished tomb as if work had suddenly been interrupted, and which I have filled in again since." He also refers to a number of objects found during clearing this tomb without any mention as to its number. Therefore, we would say that if it is T.44 there is nothing listed of those remains, thus it is most likely tomb 23; the main work in this area.[7] However these two allusions clouded the problem further until this pit may one day be unearthed again.

Two cones may have been found during the original clearance of this tomb,[8] but neither (DMC. 308, 340) belonged to Amenemhab, but clearly had strayed from their original locations, as if often the case among these tombs.[9]

**b- The scheme of decoration.**

Since the quality of limestone in the hill of Sheikh Abdel- Qurnah is very poor for sculpture, the artists of the present tomb 44 adopted the style of painted scenes and inscriptions. The well known manner in this case is to cover the unsmooth surface with a mixture of mud and coarse straw. The latter substance varies in thickness according to the roughness of the surface. Finally, a thin layer of limestone wash was laid on the surfaces and painted with colours.

The overall background colouring of the tomb is dominated by dull yellow and white. The first is mostly for the surfaces of inscriptions which were written in black and bordered in dark red. The white colour predominates in most of the scenes proper. The pale blue and green colours appear mainly with the shrines, the floral items, the offering stands and the barks, etc.

The line borders run between the registers in a broad black strip with white strips on both sides. The borders of the stelae in the eastern and western sides of the broad hall conform with a frame of patterns in different solid colours.[10] The so-called *Kheker* pattern was restricted precisely to the shrines of deified figures, since it has a religious significance in its connection as a green vegetation with resurrection.[11] However the other floral patterns are represented only by the lotus and papyrus flowers in the offering scenes.[12]

The decoration of the ceiling represents different types in both the broad hall and the long hall. The first has a winged scarab in the centre, its right side is dominated by white squares filled with light and navy blue shapes resembling grapes in bunshes.[13] But the left side differs as it is divided into plain squares with different solid colours.[14] As for that of the second hall, it is divided vertically into two parts and its remaining decoration shows diamonds in different colours.[15] No traces of inscriptions are shown on the dividing line between the two sides.[16]

The range of decoration is very limited, as the tomb lacks any great variety of subject matter. This is probably due to its small size, and to the considerable destruction on some decorative spaces, particularly ceilings and line borders. It is worth note that among many damaged tombs listed in a report by A. Fakhry about the Theban necropolis, T.44 is one of those tombs deliberately damaged by taking away a few pieces (two at least, ten at the most). The well preserved figures or heads, especially of ladies, were the prominent target of the thieves who went further by attacking the preserved tombs. From these latter, they cut away scenes and filled their places by the same substance used by the Atelier des Moulages. Thus, we do not know where the missing pieces of T.44 landed finally and whether its restoration has been done by the experts or by the tomb's robbers.[17]

However, the distribution of scenes (**pl. B**) is affected by the size of the tomb and its architectural parts. In general, the broad hall which functioned as outer room for being nearer to the external world would present mainly the ideas of this lifetime, *i.e.* occupations, amusements and incidents of career. The long hall with the shrine reflects the funerary conceptions, *i.e.* burial ceremonies, funeral procession, the mummy with sepulchral gods, offerings and the community with the living relatives and friends.[18] Those general themes were added to by the regular appearance of the scene of weighing the heart before Osiris in the Theban tombs from the 19th. Dyn., with a disregard for appropriate position especiallyin Ramesside tombs which often contain the funeral deities as well as excerpts from the Book of the Dead in their outer rooms.[19]

Consequently, a first characteristic in this respect is that scenes in T.44 are arranged according to an abridged scheme by which the broad hall was not confined solely to earthly ideas which were probably presented on the left side of the north wall before its destruction. A suggestion which is strengthened by the remaining parts of that scene of a man feeding cattle and above it another man probably plucking a goose.[20] Therefore, the religious ideas dominate the other walls of the same hall, whilst the long hall is confined closely to the religious ideas relevant to the funeral conceptions.[21]

The second feature is the lack of scenes of pastimes which are presented in many of the nobles' tombs and played the role of enjoyment for them, since their profession occupies most of their times, without leaving any for amusement. In the present writer's view, this feature was unlikely to have occured here in terms of the conservative priesthood which is represented by the owner of the tomb.

The third instructive feature relevant to the above is the representation of other priestly individuals in scenes, which illustrate obviously the career of the owner of T.44 in the Theban priesthood. Finally, the artists followed a symmetry in the depiction of scenes shown in the stereotyped appearances of the figures on the stelae in the broad hall, as well as the winged scarab on its ceiling. The same style is repeated on the niche of the long hall in the divine figures such as Osiris, Anubis, the falcon and the symbols of *ḏd*, *tit*, *wḏ3t* which play a part of protecting the deceased and preserving his body from annihilation.[22]

## Notes

[1]A. Gardiner, A. Weigall, *A Topographical Catalogue of the Private Tombs of Thebes,* London, 1913, 13, pl. VII; R. Engelbach, *A Supplement to the Topographical Catalogue of the Private Tombs of Thebes*, Cairo, 1924, pl. II; C. F. Nims, *Thebes of The Pharaohs; Pattern for Every City*, New York, 1964, 14.

[2] *Ibid., 21* ; ***PM***[2] 1/1, map. V.

[3] The state of preservation of some of the scenes mentioned in different periodicals up to 1938, seems to give us the impression that the destruction of these and probably of some others occurred most likely since that date; cf. L. Collins, *The Private Tombs of Thebes: Excavations by Sir Robert Mond 1905 and 1906*, ***JEA*** 62 (1976), 34-5 n.18.

[4]M. Abdul- Qader, *The Development of the Funerary Beliefs and Practices Displayed in the Private Tombs of the New Kingdom at Thebes*, Cairo, 1966, 10.

[5] See the plan of T.44 in ***PM***[2] 1/1, 80 ; for the plan types see ; M. Abdul- Qader, *op.-cit.*, passim. & cf. N. de G. Davies, A. Gardiner, *The Tomb of Amenemhat* (N 82), London, 1915, 11 .

[6] See chapter 2, pl.13.

[7] L. Collins, *op. cit.*, 19, 34, 40; cf. the Mond' ***MSS*** (unpublished).

[8] L. Collins, *op. cit.*, 35; N. de G. Davies, M. F. L. Macadam, *A Corpus of Inscribed Egyptian Funerary Cones*, Oxford, 1957.

[9] Examples of this, cf. (*e.g.*) L. Manniche, *Lost Tombs: A Study of Certain Eighteen Dynasty Monuments in the Theban Necropolis*, London, 1988, 3- 12; J. Kondo, *Inscribed Funerary Cones from Dra*ᶜ *Abu al-Naga*, ***Orient*** 28 (1992), 111- 23.

[10] Cf. P. Fortova- Samalova, *Egyptian Ornament*, London, 1963, pl. 95, 189.

[11] M. Abdul- Qader, *op. cit.*, 49.

[12] For the floral frieze; see E. Mackay, *Borders of Lotus and Grapes in Ancient Egypt*, ***AE***, (1921), part II, 39- 41.

[13]Cf. G. Jéquier, *Décoration Egyptienne: Plafonds et Frises Végétales du Nouvel Empire Thébain*, Paris, (1911), pls. XXIX, XXX; P. Fortova- Samalova, *op. cit.*, pl. 33, 111-113, 115

[14] *Ibid.*, pl.2, 3, 6; pl. 1, 2.

[15] Cf. G. Jéquier, *op. cit.*, pl. V; Fortova- Samalova, *op. cit.*, pl. 9, 25; pl. 12, 40,41.

[16] Cf. G. Jéquier, *op. cit.*, pl. VII.

[17] See A. Fakhry, *A Report on the Inspectorate of Upper Egypt*, ***ASAE*** 46, (1947), 32, 33.

[18]Also the broad hall corresponds with the reception room in the private house , while the long one represents the private appartment of it; See A. Badawy, *A History of Egyptian Architecture III* , Berkeley, 1968, 409.

[19] N. de G. Davies, A.Gardiner, *op. cit.*, 17-8.

[20] See pl.1.

[21] Cf. ***PM***$^2$ 1/1, 464- 471.

[22] M. Abdul- Qader, *op. cit.*, 52-3.

# Chapter 2

# Scenes and Inscriptions of the Broad Hall

## Scenes and Inscriptions of the Broad Hall

### 1- The entrance:

Scenes of the two thicknesses in the entrance have disappeared at the right side, whilst that on the left has only traces of Re-Horakhti. The surfaces of the two thicknesses as well as the ceiling are covered by the restoration cement, while the inscriptions are completely lost.

### 2- The broad hall:

**a-** The left half :

1- *North Wall* (**pl. 1, 2a**):

It is mostly damaged except one remaining fragmentary scene of a man feeding three cattle, and above it another one plucking geese. Inscriptions also here are completely lost.

2- *East Wall* (**pls. 2b, 3, 4; 2c, 5**):

It is dominated by five scenes and a painted [stela?] distributed on two registers. The left and right pairs are separated by a vertical block border, and are separated horizontally by three solid border lines.

The upper register on the left shows the deceased wearing a pleated kilt, standing and adoring Re- Horakhti. Wearing a white garment with crossed lines, the god is seated in a shrine, holding the *w3s-* scepter. A bouquet of lotus blossoms and papyrus is slightly bending towards him. The shrine is decorated with a cavetto cornice and above it is a frieze of uraei with sun disks. The throne of the god is entirely covered by coloured squares and rectangles. Between the deceased and the god stands an offering table loaded with food, and a floral "collar".

The text (**No. 1**) runs above the deceased as follows:

(1) *i3w n.k Rc- Ḥr 3ḫty, nṯr- c3, nb pt t3,* (2) [*(i)n wcb n ḥ3t Imn*][1], *sš,* (3) [ *ḥwt nṯr n*][2] *Imn, Imn-*(4) *m-ḥb m3c ḫrw.*

(1) Praise to you Re- Horakhti, great god, lord of heaven and earth, (2) by the priest in front of Amon, the scribe (3) of the temple of Amon, Amen-(4)em-hab, justified....

And above Re-Horakhti:

(5) [*Rc Ḥr 3ḫty*] (6) [*nṯr c3*] (7) *nb* [ *pt* ]. [3]

(5) Re- Horakhti (6) great god (7) lord of heaven.

The lower register of the same side shows similar action by the deceased, but in front of Atum this time. The features are mostly repeated except the dress of Atum, who wears the double crown, a short kilt and holds the *w3s*- scepter. Nine columns of text accompany these figures, and distributed as follows:

Above the deceased (**No. 2**):

(1) *i3(w) n.k p3 nb imnty* *(sic)* [4] *Itm* (2) *it nṯrw di.f* [*q*]*rst nfrt* *(sic)* (3) *ḫr imnt(y) n k3 n* (4) *wcb n ḥ3t Imn, sš* (5) *ḥwt- nṯr n Imn, Imn-* (6) *m-ḥb*.

(1) Praise to you , lord of the westerners, Atum (2) Father of the gods. May he give a good burial (3) in the west, for the *k3 of* (4) the priest in front of Amon, scribe (5) of the temple of Amon, Amenemhab.

Above Atum:

(7) *Itm*, (8) *nb t3wy, Iwnw*, (9) *nṯr* < *c3*> *nb pt(?)*.

(7) Atum, (8) lord of the two lands, the Heliopolitan, (9) <great> god, lord of heaven (?).

The right half of the same wall is badly damaged, especially its upper register. We can recognize only the deceased standing on the right and offering to a god (?). Apart from a small part of the god's shrine, the scene is completely vanished with its inscriptions. The lower register is much better as it represents the dead man offering incense and libation by holding the *hst*- jar in his right hand and the brazier in the left one. The seated god in his shrine this time is Thoth. The bouquet of flowers and the offering stand exist here at the same places similar to the left side, with one difference appears on the offering stand which does not carry ample quantity of offerings.

The inscriptions of the lower register run above the deceased as follows (**No. 3**):**

(1) *irt sntr qbḥt n k3 n* (2) *Ḏḥwty ḫnty Ḥsrt* (3) *irt wcb n ḥ3t Imn* ,(4) *Imn -m- ḥb*.

(1) Making censing and libation for the *k3* of (2) Thoth chief of Hesret, (3) made (by) the priest in front of Amon, (4) Amenemhab.

And in front of Thoth; the text reads:

(1) *Ḏḥwty nb* [............].

(1) Thoth , lord of [..........] (city).

It is worth noting that in the middle of this wall existed a scene; probably of the mountain of the west, part of which is still preserved in a red colour. It is most likely that the Hathor cow was once shown emerging from the mountain and worshipped by the deceased. Below this scene are the traces of possibly a painted stela; since only part of the cavetto cornice and the left jamb remain. [5]

3- *South Wall* (**pls. 6, 7, 8a, 9- 16**):

It is relatively rich in scenes and figures as well as inscriptions. It is divided into two registers. Starting from the left, on the upper register are two standing figures of the deceased followed by his wife in an attitude of adoration. A bouquet of lotus and papyrus flowers stands before the deceased, while his wife is holding another bouquet in her left hand. Before them are a tripod table of offerings, and two rows (each on the sky sign) of the falcon-headed souls of Buto and the jackal-headed souls of Nekhen with a baboon following each row. Before the souls, at the end of the scene is the prow of the bark of Re with the goddess Maat and a standing figure facing the god in his shrine. The remaining part of the bark rightwards and the end of the scene are lost. The scene has also lost many patches of paint, the decoration of the border lines and most of the inscriptions. The few remaining traces above the barque are illegible.

Above the deceased and his wife, are one horizontal line and five short columns. Among the traces of signs we can distinguish the name of Re-Hor-Akhty in the horizontal one, while almost nothing can be distinguished clearly in the vertical ones (**No. 4**):

........ *(Rc?) Ḥr-3ḫty di.f .... n Wsir [..........]? t.f.*

....(Re?)-Hor-Akhty, that he may give ...... to the Osiris .... [Amenemhab..,] his wife?.

Above the falcon-headed souls the text is completely destroyed. The text above the jackal-headed souls might read as follows (**No. 5**):**

- *hnw n.k b3w P [......]nb ... mi-qd(?) im.sn?* . - Jubilating for you! The souls of Pe (Buto)... Osiris ... lord? all of them?.

The remaining signs of the vertical lines before the baboons may be read as follows (**No. 6a, b**):

6a: *imyw-htw[....]* 6b: *imyw-htw[ .... ?n]fr.*

6a: The baboo[ns...]. 6b: The [goo]d? babo[ons].[6]

The lower register consists of three different scenes. The first at the left end; shows the deceased standing and offering incense and libation before the ram-standard of Amun held by its priest, who is called Paser. The ram-standard consists of a pole ending in a lotus flower surmounted by a ram's head, as symbol of Amon, with a solar disk and uraeus above. It probably has a close personal connection with the deceased, as a priest assigned specially for the offerings for this cult of Amun's standard.[7] Between the man who offers and the standard, is an offering stand carrying a *nmst-* jar, surmounted by a lotus- blossom. Below, between this man and the stand is another lotus- blossom whose long stalk is found with a series of buds as decoration. Both men are similarly dressed with long pleated kilts each with two long tasseled belt-ends.[8] The scene has some inscriptions which are badly preserved.

The inscriptions of this scene run as follows; above the deceased offering to the ram- standard (**No. 7**):

(1) *irt sntr n k3.k p3 mdw- špsi* (2) *n Imn, di.k* (3) *n.i cḥc nfr ḥr* (4) *šms k3.k* (5a) *ḫr ḥtpt...c3 m*

( And in front of the officiant): (5b) *pr- Imn n k3 n it nṯr p3 mdw- špsi, P3-sr, m3c ḫrw.*

Before the ram-standard: (6) *p3 mdw špsi n Imn.* And behind it : (7) *wcb n p3 mdw špsi [ n Imn, P3- sr].*

(1) Making censing and libation for your *k3*, O revered standard (2) of Amon. May you give (3) to me a good lifetime in serving (4) your *k3*, having (5a) a great offering(?) in (5b) the house of Amon, for the *k3* of the divine father of the revered standard, Paser, justified. (6) The revered standard of Amon. (7) The priest of the revered standard of Amon, Paser.

The second scene shows the deceased's son ᶜA- Amon and his wife called Hathor behind him. Both are standing adoring Nefertum who is seated in a shrine with the traditional decorative and floral ornaments quoted *supra* at the east wall. An offering stand is between the man and the god with a lotus blossom and lotus bud beneath the stand. The scene bears 11 columns of inscriptions above and behind the adoring figures, while those in the shrine reveal only the god's name.

The text runs above and behind the deceased as follow **(No. 8)** :

(1) *rdi(t) i3w n Nfr- tm-* (2) *Hr Ḥknw* [9] *ḥr(y).ib* (3) *r- st3w* [10] *di.f prt- hrw (m) t ḥnqt* (4 ) *k3(w) 3pd(w) qbḥw irp* (5) [*irtt..*][11] (6) *ḫt nbt* (7) *nfrt wcbt cnḫ nṯr* (8) *imm* [ *ḫrt hrw* (9) *nt rc nb*][12] (10) [ *n k3 n* ][13] (11) *wcb sš ḥwt- nṯr n pr Imn c3-Imn m3c-ḫrw, snt.f m st ib.f šmcyt n Imn Ḥtḥr, m3c- ḫrw.*

(1) Giving praises to Nefertum (2) Hor- Hekenw (who) dwells in (3) Ro- setow, may he give offerings of bread and beer, (4) oxen, fowl, libations, wine (5) and [ milk ],(6) every (7) good thing on which a god may live (8, 9) [ daily ] (10) [for the *k3*] of (11) the priest, scribe of the temple of Amon, ᶜA-Amon, justified. His sister, his favourite, chantress of Amon, Hathor, justified.

Above the god in the shrine, the text reads:

(12) *Nfr- tm nṯr- c3 nb* [ *t3wy* ] */pt* (13).... [ lost ]... [14]

(12) Nefertum, great god, lord of the two lands/ heaven. (13) ............

In the third scene, the deceased and his wife Isumut (standing behind him) adore the *hnw-* bark of Sokar. The man raises his two hands whilst the woman holds a sistrum in her right hand and a flower, probably a lotus, in the other. Before them stands an offering table. The *hnw-* bark is housed in a shrine with many of its usual ritual appurtenances, (*i.e.* the prow adorned by a gazelle turning head, holding a fish, figures of falcons, and a fan on the stern).[15]

As for the worship of Ptah-Sokar-Osiris, it is well known that Ptah- Sokar, the Memphite death god, appears in the Theban necropolis assimilated with Osiris who gave the Memphite god his way there without any representation in connection with his festival as usual. Thus, although his bark appears in the depictions very often, he lacks for his conventional texts, except very short titles. Therefore, the appearance of the Sokar-bark in T.44 reflects the funeral convention of the cult of Ptah-Sokar-Osiris in the Theban necropolis. Since the cult of Ptah spread at 45 centres in the N.K., as shown in the list of cult centres of Ptah fixed in the courtyard of tomb 158.[16]

The text above the deceased and his wife runs as follows (**No. 9**):

(1) *r<dit>*[sic] *i(3)w n k3.k Ptḥ-* (2 ) *Skr Wsir di.k šms* (3) [ *tw m mfḫ*].*k r pẖr* (4) [*inbw šms nb.f*] *n k3 n* (5) *wcb n ḥ3t <Imn>*,[ *s*]*š ḥwt nṯr* (6) *n Imn, Imn- m-* (7) *ḥb, m3c- ḫrw,* [*snt*].*f* (8) *nbt pr šmcyt n* (9) *Imn Isw- mwt, m3c(t)- ḫrw.*

(1) Giving praises to your *k3*; Ptah- (2) Sokar- Osiris, you may grant that any one may follow you, (3) on your sledge, to go around (4) the walls, (as) following his lord, for the *k3* of (5) the priest in front of < Amon >, scribe of the temple (6) of Amon, Amenem- (7) hab, justified. His sister, lady of the house, chantress of (8) Amon, Isw- mwt, justified.

**b-** The right half :-

1- *North Wall* (**pls. 17, 19a, 18, 19b, 8b, 20- 23**):

Its scenes are arranged in three registers. The upper one shows from the inner side, left, Ptah and Sekhmet in a shrine with the traditional ornaments. Before them stands an offering table and two bouquets of papyrus underneath. Then the deceased stands with hands raised. The inscriptions above and before him are mostly lost. The remaining ones read (**No. 10**):**

(1) [.....................] (2) [..................] (3) .... *rdi.f rn.i mn n ḥr imy-wrt n W3st* ..[17] (4) ....... (5) *Imn-* (6) *m- ḥb* (7) *m3c- ḫrw.*

(1) [......] (2) [.....] (3) ..... may he allow my name to abide in the west of Thebes .... (4) ...(5) Amen- (6) em-hab (7) justified.

The other part of this register represents the deified figures of Amenophis I and ᶜAhmose Nefertere seated in a shrine; he wears the *3tf*- crown as Osiris and holds the sceptre of the royal insignia. Before them the deceased offers incense in a brazier held in his left hand, whilst the other holds a libation-vessel. Between the man and the shrine stands an offering table. Unfortunately, part of the deified figures, the offering stand and most of the man's figure as well as the libation- vessel are mutilated. Also the traditional floral bouquet was omitted in the depictions of the shrine.

It is well known that Amenophis I and ᶜAhmose Nefertere were considered as patrons of the Theban necropolis and honoured as gods of the dead, since they were the first royal patrons of the royal necropolis workmen. Their cult became a popular one in the Ramesside tombs and it seems in T.44 the only attachment with royalty.[18]

Only three columns of inscriptions appear in the shrine before the deified figures bearing their names and titles; as follows (**No. 11**):**

(1) *cnh ṉtr nfr Ḏsr- K3- Rc* (2) [ *s3- Rc*] [*Imn ḥtp*] (3)[ *ḥmt ṉtr*] *Icḥ- ms Nfrt- iry.*[19]

(1) Long live the good god Djeserkara (2) Son of Re, Amonhotep. (3) The god's wife, ᶜAhmose-Nefertere.

The text above the deceased runs as follows:**

(1) *irt snṯr qkbḥt n Wsir nsw* (2) *Ḏsr- K3- Rc, n ḥmt nṯr n Imn* (3) *Icḥ- ms Nfrt- iry rdi.sn n.i* (4) *imntt*[sic] *n i3w(t)*] *nfr* [......] (5) [.......] *n k3 n Wsir sš* (6) *ḥwt nṯr nt Imn, Imn-* (7) *m- ḥb, m3c- ḫrw, nbt pr [...].*

(1) Making censing and libation to Osiris; the king (2) Djeser-ka-Ra, (and) the god's wife of Amon (3) ᶜAhmose- Nefertari , (that) they may give to me (or; allow me) (4) the west (?) [after] good [old age] (5) to the *k3* of Osiris ; the scribe (6) of the temple of Amon, Amenemhab, justified, and the lady of the house, [...].

The second register is mostly mutilated, while its inscriptions have completely vanished. The remaining depictions show only part of the deceased and his wife seated on backless chairs before an offering table. In front of them stands a priest (probably, a *Sem-priest*, since part of the funeral adze is shown in his hand). Behind the priest are the remains of two rows of seated relatives with an offering table before each one. They are most likely the sons and daughters of the deceased since the word *s3.f* ( his son) appears over the third man of the first line. Only part of two names of these can be read as follows (**No. 12**):

- *it nṯr n Imn [ N.* Lost *][* title , lost*] Imn- ḥtp.-* The divine father of Amon, [......]; [......], Amonhotep.

The third register is relatively much better preserved compared with the second. It also resembles the second one in most of its details. It shows, however, the couple seated also on backless chairs and an offering stand with an ample quantity of food in front of them. The deceased holds in his right hand the *ḫrp-* scepter, while nothing can be seen in the wife's hands since her upper part is partially mutilated. The priest who stands before the couple here is their son ᶜA- Amon. He is depicted bald, wearing a leopard skin and offering them incense and libation. Two rows of relatives dominate the other part of the register with an offering stand before each of them.

While traces of the relatives' names in this register can hardly be read, the text above the seated couple and their son is very clear and runs as follows (**No. 13**):

(1) *Wsir sš ḥwt nṯr* (2) *n Imn wcb n ḥ3t* (3) *Imn , Imn-* (4) *m- ḥb, m3c-* (5) *ḫrw. nbt pr [šm3cyt]* (6) *n Imn m* (7) *Ipt- Swt* (8,9) *Isw mwt m3ct-ḫrw* (10) *ir(t) snṯr qbḥw n Wsir* (11) *wcb n ḥ3t Imn, Imn- m-* (12) *ḥb, m3c- ḫrw, in s3.f sš* (13) *iqr, wcb cwy, wcb* (14) *n ḥ3t Imn, c3- Imn* (15) *m3c- ḫrw n W3st.*

(1) Osiris, scribe of the temple (2) of Amon, priest in front of (3) Amon, Amen- (4) em-hab, (5) justified. The lady of the house , [chantress] (6) of Amon in (7) Karnak, (8,9) Isw-mwt, justified. [10] Making incense (and) libation to Osiris, (11) priest in front of Amon, Amen- (12) em-hab, justified, by his son (13) the excellent scribe, pure of hands, the priest (14) in front of Amon, ᶜA- Amon, (15) justified, of Thebes.

2- *West Wall* ( **pls. 24- 27**):

This wall carries a mostly damaged stereotyped stela with entablature. It originally showed the deceased adoring on a large scale. The remaining part of its vaulted top shows the deceased playing the game of draughts *Snt.* In fact, the depiction of the *Snt*-game which was attested from the Old Kingdom became a popular scene in the Ramesside tombs since the reign of Ramesses II. It has no existence, as far as I know, in those of the 18 th. Dynasty.[20] Playing the game here against an imaginary opponent has a funerary significance since it guarantees the deceased a secure path in the netherworld, as reflected by the meaning derived from *Snt*; to pass or to go by. And also to give his spirit the rebirth that was a precondition of eternal life and happiness.[21]

At the sides of the stela, the deceased appears on a smaller scale surmounted by a *dd*- pillar with the *3tf*- crown at its top. On the right side of the stela, he carries the *dd*- sign on his right arm and a pectoral sign on his left one. On the other side, he carries the *tit*-sign on the left arm while the pectoral sign is on the right arm. It is worth noting that the figures of the dead on the stela have a tail attached to the girdle which was originally restricted to the gods and kings. Then it was taken over by the king's subjects as part of their funerary costume, because they believed that they could receive benefits through the mystical power of the king if they identified themselves with him.[22]

This stereotyped stela has been classified under the type which consists of two parts, and is known as the round and false door stela with a complicated type of decoration and short texts.[23]

The inscriptions of this stela are badly damaged. They are distributed in the frame as well as before and above the deceased on each side. The text can be read as follows (**No. 14a**):**

The right side; the frame: (1a) [....... lost.......] *r 3w.f, hq3 mr, wpi n ht mwt.f; di.f cq pr m hrt- ntr n(n) hnc. tw.i hr sb3w n dw3t, n k3 n Wsir, sš hwt -ntr n Imn, Imn-m-hb, m3c-hrw.*

(1a) [ Most likely the *htp di nsw* formula to ?, lord of .... ] all of it, beloved ruler, who opened his mother's womb; may he allow entry and exit from the necropolis, with no one restricting me from the doors of the netherworld, for the *k3* of Osiris, scribe of the temple of Amon, Amenemhab, justified.

Before and above the deceased: (1) [................] *in Wsir ss hwt- ntr* (2) [ *n Imn* ].... (3) [... lost...]

(4) [..........] *Imn- m-* (5) *hb m3c- hrw.*

(1)[.....] by Osiris, scribe of the temple (2)[of Amon] (3)[...lost..] (4)[.....] Amenem- (5) hab , justified.

The left side; the frame (**No. 14b**): (1a) *[Imn-Rc]-Hr-3hty [ntr] cnh, pr m nnw [shd] dw3t m [iry.f, di.f [ fh?] hr imy- wrt n [k3 n] Wsir, wcb m h3t Imn, Imn- m- hb, m3c- hrw.*

(1a) [ Probably a *ḥtp di nsw* formula to Amon] Re-Hor-Akhty-Atum-Khepri, the living [god] (who) came from the primaeval waters, [illuminating] the netherworld, with his eyes, may he grant to [depart?] on the western side, for the *K3* of Osiris, the priest in front of Amon, Amenemhab, justified.

Before and above the deceased: (1) [.........] *nb? nḥḥ in Wsir ḥsi c3 n* (2) *[ nṯr*...[lost] .... *wcb ?]* (3) *sš ḥwt- nṯr n Imn* (4) *wcb [n] ḥ3t Imn* (5) *Imn- m- ḥb, m3c- ḫrw.*

(1) [........] lord? (of) eternity, by Osiris , the greatly praised one of ... (2) [the god....[lost]...... priest] (3) scribe of the temple of Amon, (4) the priest [in] front of Amon (5) Amenemhab, justified.

3- *South Wall* ( **pls. 33a, 28- 31**):

It consists of two registers; the upper is completely lost except some fragmentary scenes, while the lower one is better conserved. Therefore, we can only see fragments in the upper register; one at the top right corner has scales with a lost text above and two figures at the bottom ( most likely the deceased and his wife) before a god's shrine of which the base only is left. At the left side of the same register are fragments of a god housed in his shrine. Although this register now is almost completely lost, it is difficult to adopt the description of ***PM*** which refers to the deceased and wife before assessors in shrines (not now preserved?).[24]

The remaining inscriptions now visible on this register are difficult to read (**No. 15a, b**). This has been complicated by modern errors in replacing some fragments on the wall. The reasonable reconstruction of these texts has to rely in large part on Mond's ***MSS*** and Kitchen's copy - neither of whom could give their true location. However, Text 15(a) partly survives on a plaster fragment wrongly placed over the right-hand scene (with the scales), instead of in the upper part of the left-hand scene. Text (15.a) also now has(or had) 5 lines, not 4 lines. Lines 1- 2 run from right to left, and lines 3- 5 run from left to right as follows:

(1) *Inpw ḫnty sḥ- nṯr* (2) ...*m?*... (3) *rdi(t) i3w* <*n*>[sic] *k3.k p3* (4) *nḏty Inpw ḫnty sḥ- nṯr wcb cwy ḏsr k3t ḥny sšt3* (5) *n Wnn- nfr didi šsp*...

(1) Anubis (who) is in front of the god's booth. (2) .......m?.......... (3) Giving praises (to) your *k3,* O (4) protector, Anubis (who) is in front of the god's booth, pure of hands, holy in works (*i.e.* embalming) , chief of secrets (5) of Onnophris (who) grants acceptance....

A large part of Text 15(b) is still preserved in a piece of plaster which has been accidentally mounted upside-down at the bottom of the left hand scene, instead of at the top. The heavy border-line was actually from the top border-lines of this scene, not from the bottom border. Text 15(b) reads:

(1) *n k3 n Wsir* (2) *sš ḥwt nṯr* (3) *n Imn, Imn- m-*(4) *ḥb* (5) *m3c-ḫrw m [ḥtp?]* (6) *snt.f mri(t).f* (7) *n st <ib>.f*[sic] , *nbt- pr, šmcyt n Imn m Ipt-<swt> ḥr s3 šmc, Isw- mwt, m3c- ḫrw.*

(1) For the *K3* of Osiris, (2) scribe of the temple (3) of Amon, Amenem- (4) hab, (5) justified in [peace?] (6) His sister, his beloved, (7) his favourite, lady of the house, the chantress of Amon in Karnak, on the south phyle, Isw- Mut, justified.

The lower register shows at its left end a pyramid-tomb with a simple corniched door-framing; pillars flank the door which is painted in yellowish colour to indicate wood and a stela was probably placed in front. The edge of this scene abuts on that of the doorway of the long hall, leaving no room to show the desert.[25]

Before the tomb stands the god Anubis who is supporting the mummy of the deceased whose head is surmounted by a scented cone of fat and a lotus blossom. In front of these two figures is an ample variety of offerings presented by a whole host of relatives, mourners, officiants and priests who are facing from the other part of the register towards the left. They hold in their hands vases, scroll and sticks. A text of 22 lines is arranged in this register as follows **(No. 16)**:

Above Anubis and the mummy: (1) *Inpw* (2) *ḫnty* (3) *sḥ- nṯr.*

(1) Anubis (who) (2) is in front of (3) the god's booth.

Above the officiants, mourners and priests :

(4) *Wsir wcb* (5) *n h3t Imn* (6) *Imn- m- ḥ3b, m3c- ḫrw.*(7) *cḥc.k, ḥr* (8) *šcyt n r-* (9) *st3w nḏ- ḥr.* (10) *[k] ḥ3[y]* (11) *n.k Itn* (12) *r- irtw n.k cbw.k* (13) *(m) mnt. wr* (14) *swcb nnw* (15) *pri n.k qbḥw* (16) *m 3bw. nḏ- ḥr.k* (17) *m nmst mn n.k snṯr* (18) *šsp n.k bd(t)* (19) *cbw tw mdwt- nṯr wp.tw* (20) *r.k m mḏ3t n bi3 n pt irty.k.*[26]

(4) Osiris, priest (5) in front of Amon (6) Amenemhab, justified. (7) May you stand upon (8) the sand of the (9) necropolis ! (10) Greetings !(11) May Aton shine for you (12) in order that your purification be made for (13) you daily. Great is (14) the making (of) purification by the primeval waters; (15) libation goes forth for you (16) from Elephantine. Greetings with (17) the *Nemset-* vase ! Take for yourself incense, (18) receive for yourself natron. (19) May the god's words purify you, (20) let your mouth be opened by the iron chisel, and (also) your eyes.

The papyrus scroll reads: (21) *irt wpt r n Wsir, Imn- m- ḥb.*

(21) Making the opening of the mouth for Osiris, Amenembab.

The horizontal line above the officiants:

(21) *Šny-*[27] *n-Imn, Imn- m- ipt, m3c- ḫrw, s3.f wcb it hwt nṯr, Ḥry.*

(21) The *sheny* (bearer?) of Amon, Amenemopet, justified. His son, the priest, the divine father of the temple?[28], Hori.

This south wall in the present writer's view deserves two possible comments. The first one tends to consider this wall as consisting of two registers only, in contrast to ***PM***, Topographical Bibliography which refers to three.[29] This view is based on several considerations. Firstly, the symmetry of the registers in the two halves of the broad hall (*e.g.* three on the north walls, stelae on the side walls and two registers on the south walls with opposite locations; as the large register lies in the bottom at the left half and *vice versa* at the right one). Secondly, the border lines which abut the entrance to the long hall and the outer frames of the west wall have no traces for a dividing line between two registers in the upper part of this south wall. Thirdly, the sizes of the fragmentary figures left in this large upper part do not give any support to a possibility of two registers there.

The second comment on this south wall is that its two registers might form one entity of the journey to the netherworld from the funeral rites up to the judgement . Thus, the reading of this wall would be more conceivable if it starts from bottom to top.

**3- The Ceiling (pl. 32, 33b)**:

It is roughly painted with coloured squares and oval shapes within, particularly on the right side. The front centre is dominated by religious motifs of a winged scarab with a solar disk in front, flanked by two uraei wearing the *3tf*-crown. The rear of this depiction is damaged. Inscriptions **(No. 17a, b)** in three short columns flank both sides of the scarab as follows:**

The right side, Text 17(a): (1) *Nḫbt [ḥnt] t3wy.* (1) Nekhbet [lady] (of) the two lands.

(2) *ḏd- mdw in Nbt- ḥwt mk cwy(.i) m s3 ḥcw.k.*

(2) Speech by Nephtys : See, (my) arms are the protection of your body.

(3) *ḥtp- di- nsw Rc-Ḥr-3ḫty-Itm, nb t3wy, iwnw.....*

(3) A boon which the King gives (to) Re- Hor- Akhty- Atum, lord of the two lands, Heliopolitan.

The left side, Text 17(b): (1) *W3dyt nb(t) pt.* (1) Wadjet, goddess of heaven.

(2) *dd- mdw in 3st mk cwy(.i) m s3 ḥcw.k.*

(2) Speech by Isis: See, (my) arms are the protection for your body.

(3) *ḥtp- di- nsw, Wsir, ḫnty imntt, wnn nfr, ḥq3 cnḫ....*

(3) A boon which the King gives (to) Osiris , foremost of the west, Onnophris, ruler of the living (!)...

## Notes

[1] Cf. the lower register; left, line 4.

[2] Cf. *ibid.*, line 5.

[3] For further examples, see H. M. Stewart, *Egyptian Stelae, Reliefs and Paintings III*, Warminster, 1983, 17, pl.9; M. Mogensen, *Inscriptions Hiéroglyphiques du Musée National de Copenhague* , ***A.A.D.*** 8, Copenhague,1918, 20; V. L. Borchardt, *Statuen und Statuetten von Königen und Privatleuten II*, Berlin, 1925 , 178; 630.

[4] The scribe in line 1 has an apparent plural in *tyw* without a plural determinative. Therefore his *imntyw* may be either 'westerners' or poor writing for *imntt* 'west'. But in line 3 he has written *imntyw* 'westerners' instead of the correct 'west'.

[5] Cf. A. Lhote, *Les Chefs-d'Oeuvre de La Peinture Egyptienne,* Paris, 1954, pl. 136; N. de G. Davies, *The Tomb of Nefer- Hotep at Thebes*, New York, 1933, 65-6, pl. LIV; R. O. Faulkner, *Book of the Dead,* (ed. by C. Andrews), London , 1993, 186-7.

[6] Cf. ***Wb.*** II, 504: 12.

[7] For this cult at the Madinet Habu temple of Ramesses III; see ***KRI*** V,139- 140, list 16; B. Bruyere, *Mert Seger à Deir Al- Medineh*, Paris, 1929, 80, n.3; H. Nelson, U. Holscher, *Work in Western Thebes 1931-33*, Chicago, 1934, 48- 50.

[8] Cf. *ibid.*, fig. 21.

[9] See for this complete name; H. Bonnet, ***Reallex.*** 510; ***LA*** IV, 38.

[10] The name of the Memphite necropolis which was given later to others ; *e.g.* Abydos, Athribis. See H. Bonnet, *op. cit.*, 642; ***LA*** V, 303-9.

[11] In most of the offering texts, as far as I know, wine is followed by milk; see W. Barta, *Aufbau und Bedeutung der Altägyptischen Opferformel*, Gluckstadt , 1968, 88, 89, 95, 110, 113,115, 116-7, 119, 138, 141, 143, 164, 165, 174, 177, 187, 188, 196, 205, 212; cf. N. de G. Davies, *The Tomb of Amenemhat* ( N 82), London, 1915, pl. 5.

[12] R. O. Faulkner, ***C.D.*** 203.

[13] Cf. W. Barta, 164, Bitte 2/b; G. Maspero, *Rapport sur une Mission en Italie,* ***Rec. Trav.*** 4 (1883), 147.

[14] We have also two probable suggestions depending on the available space for columns above Nefertum. The first might form two columns as: .... *nb t3 d̲sr, pri, m 3ht.* (... lord of the sacred land, who comes forth from heaven). The second for only one column to the word *pt* (heaven ). Cf. B. G. Ockinga, Y. Al- Masry, *Two Ramesside Tombs at El- Mashayikh II*, Sydney, 1990, 22-3, text 124; 1-2, pl. 33; J. V. d'Abbadie, *Deux Tombes Ramessides à Gournet- Mourrai*, Le Caire , 1954, 53b.

[15] M. Abdul-Qader, *The Development of the Funerary Beliefs and Practices Displayed in the Private Tombs of the New Kingdom at Thebes*, Cairo, 1966, 233.

[16] G. A. Gaballa, K. A. Kitchen, *The Festival of Sokar*, ***OR*** 38, 1969, 4, fig. 1/iii; A. Hermann, *Das Grab eines Nachtmin in Unternubien,* ***MDAIK*** 6 (1936), 29, pl. 5b; ***PM***[2] 1/1, 268-9.

[17] ***KRI*** III, 721-2.

[18] M. Abdul-Qader, *op. cit.*, 79; Bonnet, *op. cit.*, 20; J. Černý, *Le Culte d'Amenophis 1er chez les Ouvriers de la Nécropole Thébaine,* ***BIFAO*** 27 (1927), 159ff.

[19] For the various titles of Amenophis I and ᶜAhmose- Nefertary; cf. J. Cerny, 167, 174-5; ***KRI*** III, 567, 576, 583, 585, 604, 612, 616, 647, 657.

[20] M. Abdul-Qader, *op. cit.*, 253- 4.

[21] W. Decker, *Sport and Games of Ancient Egypt*, trans. by A. Guttman, American University Press, Cairo, 1993, 129.

[22] For another examples added to this rare one, see A. Wilkinson, *Ancient Egyptian Jewellery*, London, 1971; H. El-Saady, *The Reign of Sety I*, (Unpublished Ph. D. Thesis; in Arabic), Alexandria, 1989, 33; Idem., *A Fragmentary Monument from Heliopolis*, (forthcoming in ***ASAE*** ).

[23] M. Abdul- Qader, *op. cit.*, 39; 46, 47.

[24] ***PM***[2] 1/1, 84; (7)i,ii.

[25] N. M. Davies, *Some Representations of Tombs from the Theban Necropolis*, ***JEA*** 24 (1938), fig. 22(1:6), 35, 39; A. Badawy, *Le Dessin Architectural chez les Anciens Egyptiens*, Le Caire, 1948, 226, (fig. 285 [1]).

[26] E. Otto, *Das Ägyptische Mundöffnungsritual I*, 58-9; 26 d,e.

[27] For the title '*šny- n-* (god)'; see ***Wb.*** IV, 503:11,12. Legrain suggested 'guardian', but he had confused *šny* and *šnc*. In the context he quotes (CGC. 42189), 'bearer' would fit better. Further suggestions would be welcome, see, M. G. Legrain, *Le Logement et Transport des Barques Sacrées et des Statues des Dieux dans Quelques Temples Egyptiens*, ***BIFAO*** 13 (1917), 39 and n. 3.

[28] The sign here could be either for 'palace' as Mond transcribed, or temple ( or shrine) as concords with the deceased' career ; cf. ***WB*** I , 142; [3].

[29] ***PM***[2] 1/1, *loc. cit.*

# Chapter 3

# Scenes and Inscriptions of the Long Hall

## Scenes and Inscriptions of the Long Hall

1- *North Wall* **(pl. 34, 35a)**:

It is formed by two parts of the inner sides of the doorway of this hall; each of which has three registers in bad condition and lost texts. The right side, which abuts the east wall, shows in each register the deceased standing and receives offerings with a stick in his right hand and the *ḫrp*-sceptre in his left one. Before him is a lotus blossom and the *nmst*- jar on an offering stand. The offerer is completely lost except his hand in the middle and lower registers where he presents incense brazier and an ointment jar, respectively. The lost one on the top register is probably a libation vessel.

The left side shows in its three registers the deceased seated before an offering stand and holds a bouquet of lotus flowers in his right hand. The deceased raises a bowl in his left hand while the offerer in front of him pours from a jar. Also here the offerer's body is lost except his hand.[1] The vaulted part of the doorway shows traces of a double scene of a pair of recumbent figures of Anubis with a flagellum, facing each other.

Unfortunately, neither the latter nor the registers on the flanking walls have presented any of the inscriptions although the yellow spaces in every register with black borders formerly had texts of about eight columns each. Part of the text for the middle scene at left can be read as follows (**No. 18**):

(1) *Wsir wcb n ḥ3t* (2) *[Imn, sš ḥwt-nṯr]* (3) *Imn-m-* (4) *ḥb* (5) *m3c-ḫrw* (6)...... (7) ...... (8) *irt snṯr* ......

(1) Osiris, priest in front of (2)[ Amon, scribe of the temple] (3) Amenem (4) hab, (5) justified. (6)......

(7) ......... (8) presenting incense .......

2- *East Wall* **(pls. 35b- 38b)**:

Scenes of this wall start from the left and originally filled the whole space in one big entity, displaying the hall of judgement. The first scene depicts Anubis leading the deceased as a guide to Thoth, then Osiris at the other end of the wall. Scenes of the middle part of the wall are lost, taking away probably some of the traditional items of this scene such as Ma$^{c}$et, the balance, the monster Ammit, the squatting deities who are witnesses to the judgement.[2] The next scene shows two couples in two rows on a small scale led to Osiris by Thoth who is wearing the *3tf*-crown with uraei horns and carrying his scribal palette. At the right end of the wall is a shrine where Osiris stands in his mummified form wearing the *3tf*-crown and holding the *w3s*-sceptre; before him is the *imy-wt* fetish of Anubis.

Apparently the text above the deceased and Anubis is already affected by the loss in the middle of the wall. The rest of the text, however; runs as follows: **

(1) [....... lost ..... ] (2) .......... *[Wsir] Imn- m* (3)-*[ḥb, m3c]- ḫrw, mi ir.k* (4) ............ *nb imyw,* (5) ....... *di.tw n.k* (6) ..*[t],qbḥ(t) m b3ḥ Wnn* (7)- *nfr [ḏd].wy rn.k m* (8) *r- st3w ḥnc šmsw* (9) *Ḥr wn imntt, cwy(.i)* (10) *m nyny r šsp* (11) *scḥ.k , Wsir, Imn-m-ḥb.*

(1) [....... lost .....] (2) ......[ Osiris ] Amenem- (3) hab, justified, now come (4) ...... all who are in (5) ......, may you be given (6) ...., [bread?] and libation in the presence of Onnophris. (7) How stable is your name in (8) Re- Setau, along with the followers of (9)Horus. Opened is the west; (my) hands (10) are in greeting to receive (11) your mummy, O Osiris Amenemhab.

The completion of this text on the other side of the wall extends *ca.*12 columns at least above the couple of the upper row, Thoth and the shrine of Osiris. Unfortunately, it is mostly damaged since few signs remain; see as text ( **No. 20**).** [3]

The text above the couple of the lower row reads as follows (**No. 21**): [4]

(1) *Wsir, sš, wdḥw nsw* (2) *n nb t3wy, imy- r n nw* (3) [... lost...], *m3c ḫrw.* (4) *nbt pr šmcyt n Imn,* (5)[... lost ....]*r, m3c- ḫrw.*

(1) Osiris, scribe of the royal table (2) of the lord of the two lands, overseer of hunters (3) [Name lost], justified. (4) The lady of the house, chantress of Amon, (5)[Name ends in, *r*], justified.

As for the text in the shrine of Osiris, it consists of four columns as follows (**No. 22**):**

(1) *Wsir, ḫnty [imntyw]* (2) *wnn nfr [cnḫ?]* (3) ..... *nb [3bḏw, ḥq3 nṯrw ?]* (4) *nṯr c3* ......

(1) Osiris, foremost of [the westerners] (2) Onnophris [the living?] (3) ...... lord of [Abydos, ruler of gods ?] (4) the great god ......

It is worth commenting on the existence of the two couples before Osiris in the hall of judgement. An entensive survey for similar examples unearthed five tombs having two couples before Osiris in the scenes of the Book of the Dead. All of them are Ramesside; four from Ramesses II's reign and the fifth undated. The couples of these latter vary in their relation to the tomb owner, *i.e.* the brother and wife, the deceased and mother, or the son and his wife.[5]

The present writer is inclined to consider the couples of T.44 as the deceased and his wife in the upper row whilst the lower one is dedicated for his son and the wife. This view is based on, firstly, the titles of the son as "scribe of the royal table and overseer of hunters of Amon", which were never held by Amenemhab in his priestly career. Secondly it is not customary, as far as I know, to depict the deceased twice before Osiris in the hall of judgment either in the Ramesside private tombs or anywhere else.

3- *West Wall* ( **pls. 39- 48**):

It consists of two registers where the lower one dominates the space of two similar to those in the broad hall; *i.e.* the lower register on the south wall (left half of the wall) and the upper one on the same wall (right half of the wall). The upper register, however, is barely preserved since one of its two scenes is mostly damaged. At the inner left end, the remains show the deceased and his wife seated with a priest offering to them.[6] Further right (middle of the register), the second scene has also similar two figures who are seated on backless chairs whilst a man is offering to them and to a woman standing behind the wife. This latter is most likely their daughter since it is common to find children behind or beside their parents particularly in most of the Ramesside private tombs.[7] The right hand section of this register is almost entirely lost, leaving nothing to be described in detail.

The inscriptions of this register are completely lost except the remains of a vertical line behind the standing woman of the second scene, but belonging to the first (left) scene, and it might read as follows (**No. 23**):**

*[ Wsir, wcb n ḥ3t] Imn, sš [....] nb t3wy m pr Imn, Imn-m-ḥb, m3c-ḫrw.*

[ The Osiris, priest in front of Amon, scribe [of..... of] the lord of the Two lands in the estate of Amon, Amenemhab, justified.

The large lower register has interlocking scenes of a funeral procession. First at left, is the goddess of the west holding upright the mummy of the deceased before an ample heap of various offerings which might separate significantly between life and death.[8] Before them stand three figures, two of them as priests clad in a panther skin raising ritual implements for censing and libating. The third one holds an open blank scroll, almost all that is left, as his body is damaged taking with it probably another figure.

The text over the last figures is arranged as follows (**No. 24**):

(1) *Wsir* (2) *wcb n ḥ3t* (3) *Imn [sš ḥwt nṯr]* (4) *n Imn, Imn- m-*(5) *ḥb, m3c- ḫrw.* (6) *irt wpt- r [...]w*

(7) *[.....]m* (8) *ḥwt nbw cḥc ḥr ḫ3st* (9) *< nt> šc(t) ḥr.f* (10) *r [rsi ḥ3y]* (11) *[m t3 hrw]*(12) *[mnḫt ḥ3.f].*[9]

(1) Osiris, (2) priest in front of (3) Amon, scribe of the temple (4) of Amon, Amenem- (5) hab, justified. (6) Performing the opening of the mouth ritual for .... (7)........... in (8) the house of gold, it standing (9) on the sandy desert . His face (10) is turned towards [the south , naked (11) upon the earth on the day, (12) when the clothes are behind him].

Behind the latter scene, two lines of figures are depicted. The upper one has a row of bearers facing left and carrying burial-goods, while the lower line shows fragments of an ox and its driver as well as a man (probably a priest) with a brazier facing towards the right side to cense a catafalque. This latter interrupts the two lines and is ornamented by rows of *tit* and *ḏd* signs arranged arranged alternately. One line of inscriptions above the bearers reads (**No. 25a**):- *ḏdt.n n3 rm(t) nty ḥr ḥ3t p3 qrst, r imnt sp sn*[10] *[...] ḥsy r imnt, qrst.k m ḫft-ḥr-nb.s mi m3cty nb (?).*

Said by the people who are in front of the burial: "To the west ! to the west !O blessed one, towards the west! your burial is in the Theban necropolis ( Kheft-her-nebes ), like every just person". (or; according as you are justified).

Another line runs above and behind the man who is censing the catafalque as follows (**No. 25b**):

- *irt sntr qbḥw n k3 n Wsir sš ḥwt- nṯr n Imn, Imn- m- ḥb.*

Making incense (and) libation for the *k3* of Osiris, the scribe of the temple of Amon, Amenemhab.

The scene behind the catafalque contains another two lines of the funeral procession. The upper one starts with three priests carrying a portable shrine which resembles the tomb since Anubis is recumbent on its top. Then seven topless women and three nude young girls (some of them are most likely wife and daughters)[11] are mourning, while the last woman in the row is facing the opposite way by her position and pouring liquid from a red pot before breaking it on a heap of red potsherds on the ground. This upper row, however, ends with four booths of funerary provisions attended by two men and two women standing before them alternately.

The inscriptions of this upper line are confined on the names of the women and the young girls and arranged as follows (**No. 26**):-

- Before the first woman two names; the upper one is *ḥmt, Imn ....;* "the maid- servant, Amon[ ..lost..] ". The lower one is *ḥmt, T3- nfr(sic) hnwt;*" the maid servant, Taneferhenut ".

The third name on her kilt reads *ḥmt, Nḫt-m-(?) Mut;* "the maid servant, Nekhtem(?)mut.

The fourth name behind the first young girl is *ḥmt, Nsmwt;* "the maid servant, Nesmut ".

The fifth name behind the second young girl is *[ḥmt, Nḏm]- bḥdt;* "[the maid servant, Nedjem]behdet ".[12]

Behind the third young girl the sixth name reads *hmt, Wsr-t3-ib-Mut;* "the maid servant, Wesertaebmut ".

Above the heap of the broken pot sherds is the seventh name which reads *ḥmt, T3- ḫpš- m- ns:* "the maid servant, Takhepeshemnes", while the name above the first booth is mutilated.

The performance of the Memphite ritual of breaking pots (*sḏ- dšrw*) done by the last woman of the mourning ones is worth noting for comment. First, it was preceded by emptying their liquid which may be water either to perform the ritual of removing the foot print (*int rd*), or to represent the blood when it runs out from the body after death by the water streaming from jars.[13] Second, the depiction of breaking pots in the present tomb by a woman not by a man is typically Ramesside.[14]

The lower line includes two tow- boats with crew appearing in the top one, while only the prow and three men remain from the boat at the bottom. Behind them is a funeral barque with ornamented shrine.[15]

Above the prow of the bottom boat and the three men a text of four lines reads as follows (**No. 27**):

(1) *[n3?] srw* (2) *nty ms* (3) *p3 qrs(t)* (4) *ḥsy n [.....] Imn- m- ḥ3b, m3c- ḫrw.*

(1) [The?] officials (2) who are bringing (3) the coffin (of) (4) the blessed one [.....] Amenemhab, justified.

4- *South Wall* (**pls. 49, 54a; 50- 53; 54b- 57**):

It consists of three registers taking the shape of a vaulted stela. The first (top) one, has a stela at the centre showing in its upper half double seated figures of Osiris housed in a shrine and facing opposite directions, while Anubis is before each one at the sides. The lower half shows the *ḏd*-signs of Osiris in the middle and the *tit*-signs of Isis at the sides. Unfortunately, most of the right part of the stela as well as the two sides of the register are thoroughly destroyed.

The second register is occupied in its centre by the niche (see below), whilst the side surfaces have a stereotyped scene for the deceased offering to Ptah- Sokar- Osiris in mummified form, wearing the white crown and holding the *w3s*- sceptre.

The text on each side is mostly mutilated and runs in six columns above the figures as follows; firstly at left (**No. 28**):**

(1) *[W]sir,nb [nḥḥ], ḥq3 t3- ḏsr(??)* (2) *[?dw3] Ws[ir],[nb-nḥḥ]* (3) *[i]n Wsir, wcb n ḥ3t* (4) *[Imn],[sš] ḥwt- [nṯr]* (5) *Imn-m-ḥb,* (6) *m3c- ḫrw m ḥtp.*

(1) The Osiris, lord of eternity, ruler of the sacred land (??) (2) [?Adoring] Os[iris, lord of eternity] (3) by the Osiris, priest in front of (4) [Amon], [scribe] of the temple of (5) Amon, Amenemhab, (6) justified.

Secondly at right (**No. 29**):**

(1) *[Ptḥ] S[k]r Wsir* (2) ....... *r* (3) [..lost..] (4)[..lost..](5) [..lost..] (6)[..lost...].

(1) [Ptah]- So[k]er- Osiris (2) ...... to (3) ..lost.. (4) ..lost.. (5) ..lost.. (6) ..lost...

The third and lower register shows another damaged stereotyped scene of the deceased and his wife with offerings before them. The inscriptions are arranged in columns before and above the couple at each side. The remaining signs of the text at left read (**No. 30**): **

(1) *ḏd mdw in [ .....] Imn ......* (2)....*[ prt-nṯr]* (3) .... [..lost.. ] *cq pr m ḫrt-nṯr* (4) [..lost..] (5) *nbw nḥḥ* (6) *šmc(yt)* (7) *Imn* (8) *[Isw- Mwt],* (9) *m3c-ḫrw.*

(1) Words spoken by [....] Amon ..... (2).....[ ] (3) .... [lost..] the going forth of the god (4)[.. lost..] (5) lord of eternity (?) (6) chantress of (7) Amon, (8) [Iswmwt], (9) justified.

At right the text is badly damaged and we can distinguish the deceased's name directly before him (**No. 31**):

(1)- (3) [ lost] (4) *in.....* [lost] (5) *Imn-m-ḥb* (6) *ff.* [lost].

(1)- (3) [ lost] (4) bringing ... [lost] (5) Amenemhab, (6) ff [lost].

It is worthwhile to refer that it would be more conceivable if we read the east and west walls in opposite order to that of ***PM***. Thus we would start from the top register of the west wall to the bottom one, then we move to the east wall. This order would draw a precised picture of Amenemhab's life where he was honoured in life as priest , mourned in death by relatives and friends then welcomed in heaven by the gods.

5- *The Niche* ( **pl. 53, 54b, 55**):

Its outer surface shows remains of an entablature topped by a cornice. The rear wall includes in the middle an Osiris-emblem which has on each side the ram-standard of Amon. Above the latter is the winged falcon with *šn*- sign, whilst a bouquet of flowers stands beneath it.

The left wall of the niche has a mutilated scene which depicts the deceased in his priestly appearance before an offering stand and holding a censer. Only a few words remain from the text which runs in columns above the figures in the scenes as follows (**No. 32**):**

(1) *irt sntr qbḥ n* (2) *[Wsir....]*(3) *[ in wcb ḥ3t Imn]* (4) *[sš ḥwt-ntr n Imn]* (5) *[Imn-m-ḥb]* (6) *m3c-* (7) *ḫrw m ḫrt-ntr,m* (8) [.......].

(1) making incense and libation to (2)[ Osiris.....] (3) to the priest in front of Amon] (4) [ scribe of the temple of Amon] (5)[ Amenemhab] (6) justi- (7) fied in the necropolis, in (8) [......] .

On the right wall the scene is repeated, showing the priest Amenemhab holding a brazier and libation vase before an offering stand. A mutilated text of eight columns runs above the scene and reads as follows (**No. 33**):**

(1) *i[rt sntr qbḥ....]* (2) [..lost..] (3)... *sš wdḥw* (4) [.....lost..] (5-6) *[pr- Imn ??, ]* (7-8) *Imn-m-ḥb* (9)

*[ m3c- ḫrw].*

(1) Making [incense and libation for....] (2) [.........lost...] (3) [ by...] the scribe of the offering-table, (4) [..lost..] (5-6) [of the estate of] Amon (7-8) Amenemhab, (9) justified.

## Notes

[1] The investigation on the private tombs of the similar pattern of design to T. 44 such as tombs 17, 32, 41, 50, 53, 56, 149, 341, proved in general that there is no standard rule on what is depicted on the flanking walls, since they show various secular and religious scenes. Nevertheless, tombs nos. 41, 149, 341 which are mainly Ramesside, are more restricted in depicting in the same locations as that on T.44 either the deceased on each side or accompanied by his wife or his son with offering stand. See for the group of tombs above ***PM***$^2$ 1/1; *passim*.

[2] M. Abdul- Qader, *The Development of the Funerary Beliefs and Practices Displayed in the Private Tombs of the New Kingdom at Thebes*, Cairo, 1966, 252; cf. Pap. of Hunefer, pl. 4; in W. Budge, *The Book of the Dead of the Pap. of Hunefer, Anhai, Kerasher and Netchmet*, London, 1899; R. O. Faulkner, *Book of the Dead* ; ( ed. by C. Andrews), London, 1993, 34; E. Naville, *Das Aegyptische Todtenbuch der XVIII bis XX Dynastie*, Berlin, 1886, pl. CXXXVI, A.g.; N. de G. Davies, *Two Ramesside Tombs at Thebes*, New York, 1927, pl. XIII.

[3] It is much better to compare the whole text with that in Pap. of Hunefer as a well preserved and complete version of spell 125 at the "Hall of Judgement", see, W. Budge, *loc. cit.*, & R. O. Faulkner, *op. cit.*, 29- 34; also illustrated in pp. 14, 30, 34.

[4] For the text of the couples we would adopt fig. 21a of Kitchen (see ***JEA* 62** (1976),24), since there is no allusions to the place of fig. 21b in Mond's ***MSS*** at the scene.

[5] Cf. ***PM***$^2$ 1/1, tombs nos. 2, 31, 32, 356, 387.

[6] *Ibid.*, 84; (11) I,[1].

[7] M. Abdul- Qader, *op. cit.*, 112, pl. 39 & S. Whale, *The Family in the Eighteenth Dynasty of Egypt*, Sydney, 1989, 257.

[8] N. de G. Davies, *op. cit.*, 26.

[9] E. Otto, *Das Ägyptische Mundöffnungsritual* , 2 vols,Wiesbaden, 1960, I; 1- 3, II; 34-7.

[10] For the expression "go to the west ! go to the west !", see; G. A. Gaballa, The Memphite Tomb-Chapel of Mose, Warminster, 1977,17 & E. Luddeckens, *Untersuchungen Über Religiosen Gehalt, Sprache und Form der Ägyptidchen Totenklagen,* ***MDAIK*** 11 (1943), 132, 139, 141, 143, 145.

[11] For the mourning wife and girls, cf. as famous examples; G. Foucart, *Tombes Thébaines, Nécropole de Dira$^c$ Abu' N- Naga, Le Tombeau d'Amonmos*, Le Caire, 1935, pl. II, & N. de G. Davies, *The Tomb of the Vizier Ramose*, London, 1941, pl. XLIX.

[12] Cf. H. Ranke, ***PN*** I, 215: 13.

[13] J. Van Dick, The New Kingdom Necropolis at Memphis: A Historical and Iconographic Study, Groningen, 1993, 173- 88; Borchardt refers to the scene of breaking pots in T.44 as the only one in Theban tombs which is depicted in connection with mourning procession. But I owe to my colleague Dr. Essam A. Dabash the addition of another three possible examples (tombs nos. 13, 57, 178.) of the same scene. See L. Borchardt, *Bilder des " Zerbrechens der Krüge ",* ***ZAS*** 64 (1929), 12-3, pl. I/1; cf. E. A. Dabash, *The Execration Texts in Ancient Egypt* ( unpublished Ph. D. thesis), Alexandria, 1994.

[14] J. Van Dick, *loc. cit.*

[15] One may note that the rear barque is not of Sokar (contrary to ***PM***; see pl. 21).

# Chapter 4

# The Owner of the Tomb

## The Owner of the Tomb

### 1- Career and titles:

Amenemhab was a middle ranking priest of Amon in Thebes. His two principal titles are *wcb n ḥ3t Imn*; "the priest in front of Amon" and *sš ḥwt nṯr n Imn*; "the scribe of the temple of Amon". The first title apparently referred to his priestly service in the phyle of Amon,[1] whilst the second one refers to an administrative task at the temple of Amon [2], perhaps specifically for the offering table of Amon (Text. 33).

### 2- Members of the family:

Grandfather : Amenemopet.

Title : *šny n Imn* ; the bearer of Amon. Wife : ?.

Father : Hory.

Titles: *wcb, it-nṯr ḥwt*; the priest, the divine father of the temple.[3]

Wife:?.

Wife: Isw-mwt.

Titles: *nbt-pr, šmcyt n Imn m Ipt-swt ḥr s3 šmc* ; the lady of the house, chantress of Amon in Karnak [4] on the south phyle.

Children:

In his ***MSS*** no. 4.14; Sir R. Mond confused Amenemhab of T.44 with Amenemhat of tomb 48, who is also called Surer. He also attributed the names of sons and daughters to the latter by mistake. But the study of names in tomb 48 proved that Amenemhat's mother appears where we should expect his wife, and neither a wife nor children are ever mentioned since Amenemhat (Surer) seems to have been a bachelor.[5] Thus these names are attributed to Amenemhab since they would fit with the fragmentary names attached to the figures in the banquet and procession scenes in T.44. We would list them as follows :

I- Sons:

1- ᶜA- Amon.

Titles: *wcb, sš ḥwt- nṯr n pr Imn* ; the priest, scribe of the temple of Amon.

Wife : Hathor. Title : *šmcyt n Imn* ; chantress of Amon.

2- Amenhotep.

Title : *it nṯr n Imn* ; the divine father of Amon. Wife : ?.

3- [Amenmose?] :

Titles : *sš wdḥw- nsw n nb- t3wy, imy- r n nw n Imn* ; scribe of the royal table of the lord of the two lands, overseer of hunters of Amon.[6]

Wife: ?. Titles: *nbt- pr, šmcyt n Imn*; the of the lady of the house, chantress of Amon.

II- Daughters:

All of their names are preceded by *šmcyt* (chantress) which is considered as a title rather than a name.[7] We would list the remaining fragmentary ones amongst the available six, which were names commonly known at the Ramesside Period .[8]

1- Name lost. 2- Nefertery.[9] 3- Tamy(t).[10]

4- Iryt- nefret.[11] 5- Name lost. 6- Name lost.

It is worth observing that the existence of the priest Paser tends to in relation to priestly service as " the divine father of the revered standard of Amon" , rather than for family relationship since there is no allusion to any such family link between him and Amenemhab.[12]

To comment on the representation of Amenemhab's family ; it is noticeable that the texts usually refer either to his wife or his son's wife as *snt* (sister). This might imitate the natural relationship of the royal marriage and also the new status and role which is received by the wife as "a sister".[13]

The chief role of his sons was to perform the funerary offerings for their parents.[14] But this role seems to be more restricted to the eldest son who might be here ᶜA-Amon since he is the only son who inherited his father's main titles. We would also notice that the nuclear family of Amenemhab (*i.e.* wife, sons and their wives, daughters) have a priestly career or honorific attachment to it, as shown from their titles.

As for the relatives who are represented in banquet scenes and even in procession scenes, their condition is similar to that of most of the private tombs; the essence of the difficulty is to tell which are represented in the tomb. On the other hand, being seated or standing in a row one behind the other before the deceased and his wife, they seem to form an "open group" meeting which was restricted mainly to relatives.[15]

## Notes

[1] See ***LA*** IV, 1089; ***LA*** VI, 389; H. Kees, *Das Priestertum im Ägyptischen Staat, Leiden*, 1953, 301-2; cf. A. M. Roth, *Egyptian Phyles in the Old Kingdom*, ***SAOC*** 48, Chicago, 1991, 83-4; ***Urk.*** IV, 1950.

[2] G. Lefebvre, *Histoire des Grands Prêtres d'Amon de Karnak*, Paris, 1929, 301-2; S. Sauneron, *Les Prêtres de l'Ancienne Egypte*, Paris, 1957, 55-8.

[3] ***PN*** I ; 245: 18, 21 .

[4] *Ibid.*, 46, [27].

[5] See T. Säve- Söderbergh, *Tomb 48 of Amenemhat (Surer)*, 34-5.

[6] The name of this son might be Amenmose of tomb 149 (also Ramesside) since this is the only the Ramesside tomb, as far as I know, whose owner's titles coincide with those in T.44 ; see A. Gardiner, A. Weigall, *A Topographical Catalogue of the Private Tombs of Thebes*, London, 1913, 30-1, & ***PM***[2] 1/1, 260.

[7] *Šmcyt* was taken as a personal name once only at the Middle Kingdom. As for the daughters of Amenemhab; all of them were chantresses of Amon except who was of Mut. See ***PN*** I, 327: 25, & ***LA*** IV, 1102.

[8] For further names and references; see ***PN*** I, *passim.*

[9] Cf. G. Legrain, *Recherches Généalogiques*, ***Rec.Trav.*** 31 (1909), 212: 10, & ***PN*** I, 201: 16.

[10] Cf. E. von Bergmann, *Inschriftliche Denkmäler*, ***Rec.Trav.*** 12 (1892),18, xx, & G. Daressy, *Les Temples d' Abydos*, ***Rec.Trav.*** 21(1899), 8, & ***PN*** I, 357: 5.

[11] *Ibid.*, 42: 5.

[12] *Ibid.*, 117: 12, 13 .

[13] S. Whale, *The Family in The Eighteenth Dynasty of Egypt*, Sydney, 1989, 273- 4.

[14] *Ibid.*, 274.

[15] See *Ibid.* , 1- 3.

# Conclusions

## Conclusions

The major problem to solve in studying T.44 is in fact its dating to a specific period of the Ramesside era, particularly in the 19th. Dynasty. Since the inscriptions have no allusions to any ruling pharaoh, the clues we must rely on naturally have different scope, wider or more restricted, to indicate the date in time which we would suggest.

Firstly, most of the "hall of judgement" scenes in these tomb-chapel (*i.e.* leading the deceased by Anubis, weighing the heart, presentation before Osiris) are Ramesside. But dated examples are mainly attributed to the time of Ramesses II. Their depiction, moreover, appears at its best in the early 19th. Dynasty, especially Ramesses II's reign when it reached its peak. By then, tomb-decoration tended to be dominated by long series of afterlife scenes, rather than secular scenes. This latter feature distinctively distinguishes T.44.

Secondly, a scrutiny of specific detailed phenomena is helpful in dealing with the issue of dating T.44. These include: (a) The representation of Thoth in the judgement-scene which was mainly restricted to the early 19th. Dynasty. (b) The adoption of end-wall stelae in the broad hall exists in a wide time-range from the late 18th. Dynasty up to the reign of Ramesses II. (c) The existence of another couple, apart from the deceased and his wife, before Osiris in the hall of judgement is attributable to tombs of the time of Ramesses II. (d) Also, the depiction of figures either adoring or offering on each side of the doorway into the inner parts of the tombs is mostly an early 19th. Dynasty feature. (e) The replacement of the deceased's biography by afterlife depictions, reached its peak as a trend in Ramesses II's reign.

These preceding lines of evidence would allow us to reach a degree of certainty concerning the dating of the tomb which I am inclined to place in the reign of Ramesses II.

The distribution of scenes was conditioned mainly by the size of the tomb, careless preparation of the walls as well as the profession and rank of the owner of T.44. These elements affected the possibility of depicting scenes according to the use and significance of each part of the tomb which was dominated by religious scenes at the expense of secular ones, since they were blended in a single harmonious scheme. Nevertheless, scenes of afterlife and the funeral are depicted on a large scale when compared to subordinate scenes of worshipping gods. This sort of imbalance would not allow us to establish clear criteria for the placement of the scenes of T.44. But in part, we would consider the order of registers of the south wall at the right side of the broad hall, to be read from the lower register to the top one and from right to left for them both. Scenes of the long hall, however, would start from the right side of the lower register up to the upper one, of its west wall. Then on the east wall, the scenes progress from left to right, so that the whole hall focuses the niche and its scenes at the rear of this hall of the tomb-chapel.

Finally, the function of T.44 both as an eternal habitat of the deceased and as a chapel for the funerary cult raises one particular problem in studying T.44: due to the undiscovered burial shaft where the mummy of Amenemhab ought to rest. Despite this lack, the present writer would consider it a tomb-chapel of double functions since it seems to fulfill both purposes.

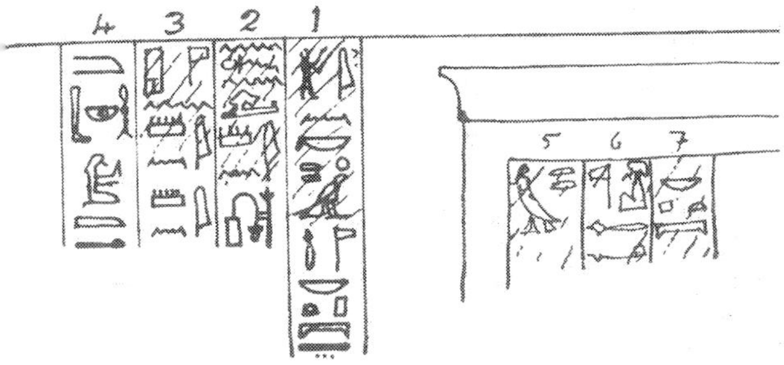

Text 1

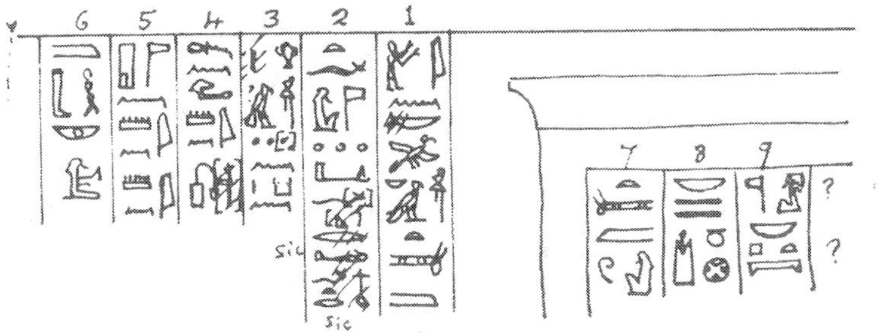

Text 2

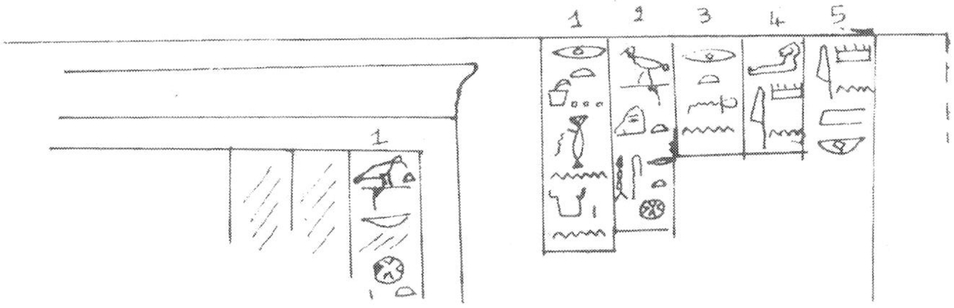

Text 3

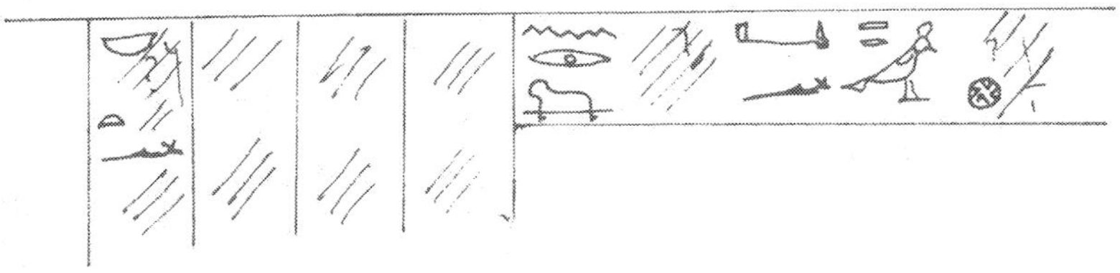

Text 4

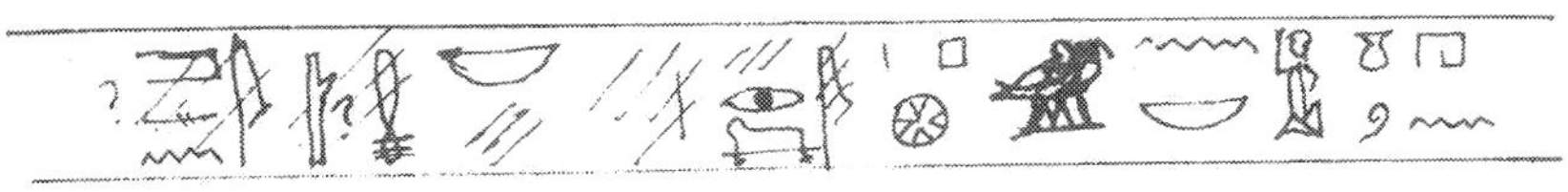

Text 5

Text 6b

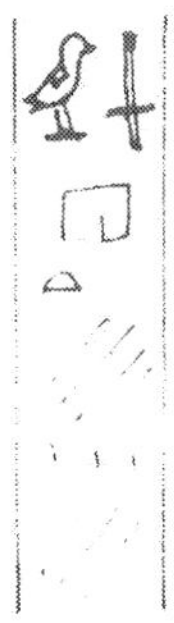

Text 6a

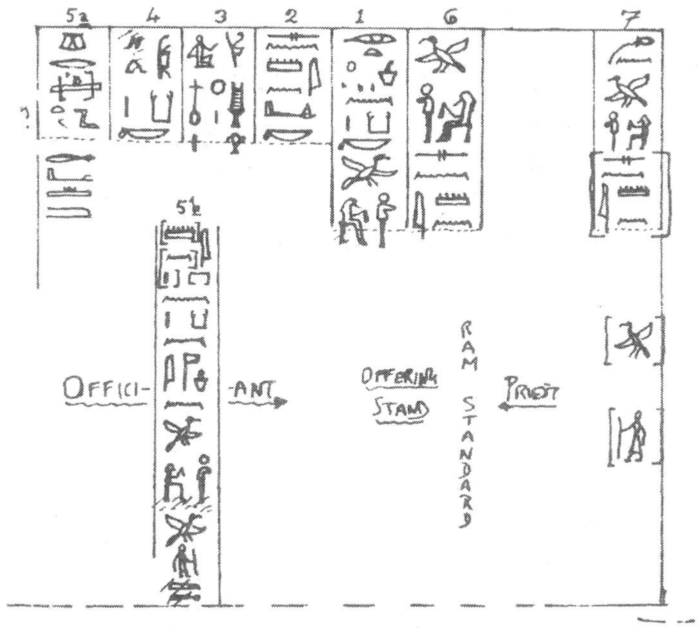


**Text 7**

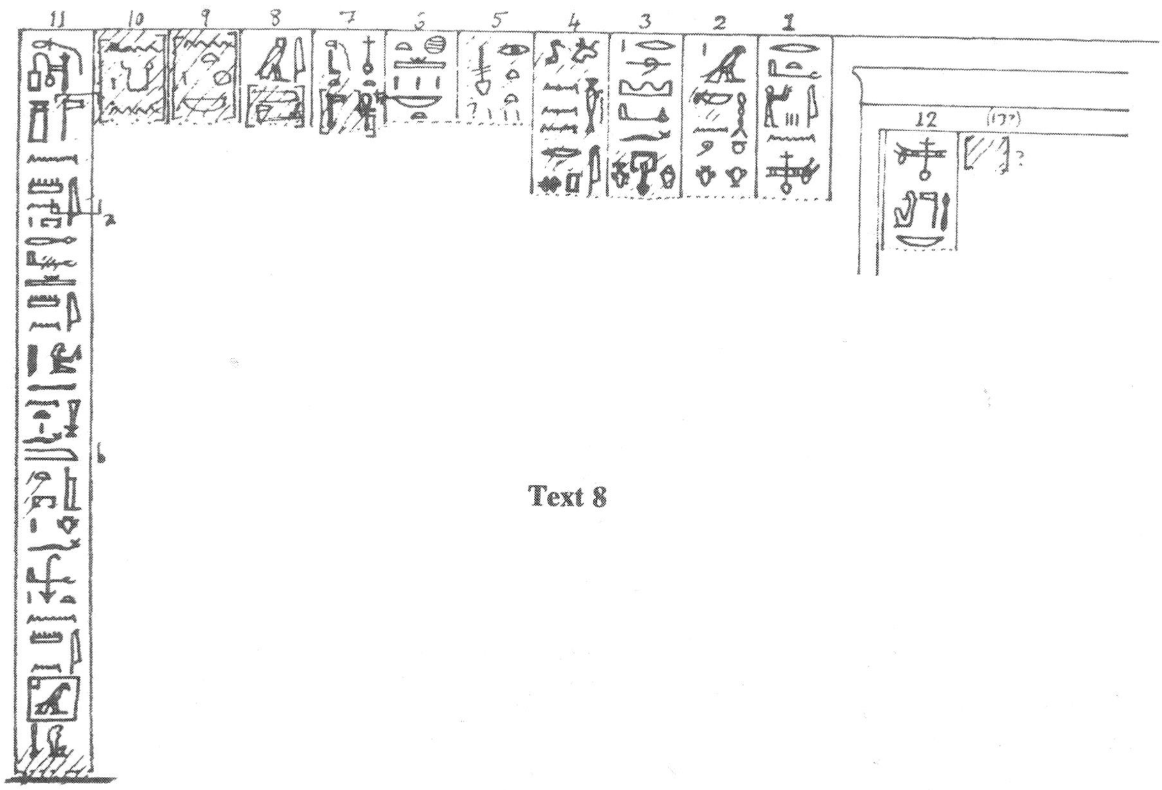

**Text 8**

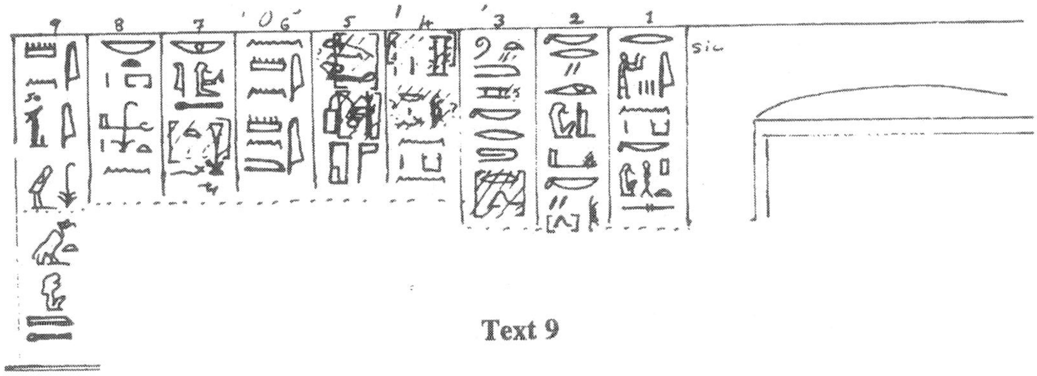

Text 9

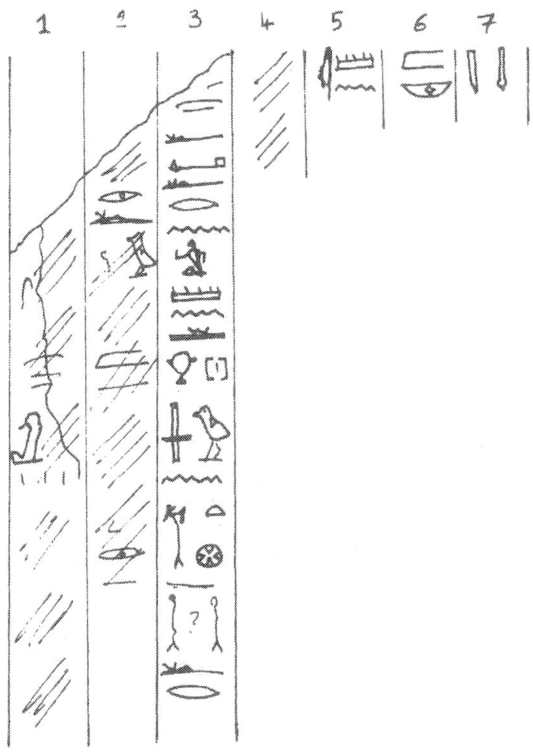

Text 10

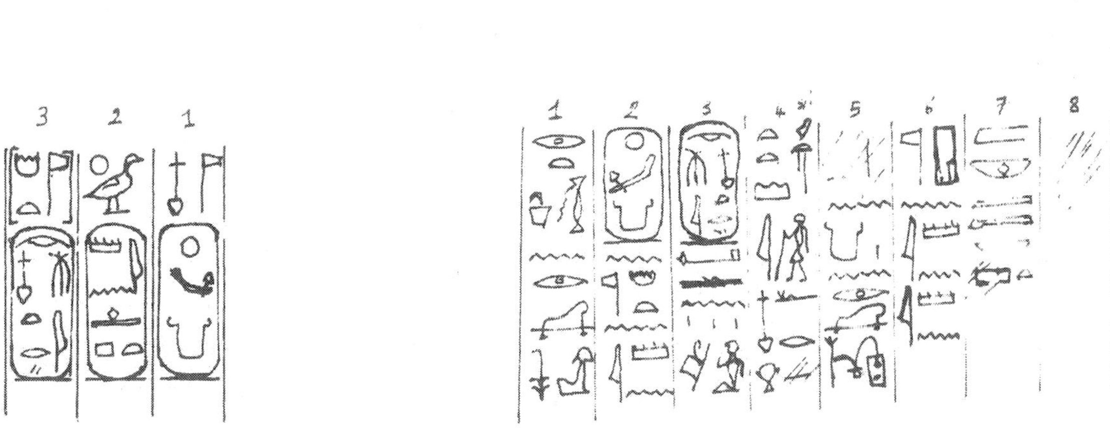

Text 11

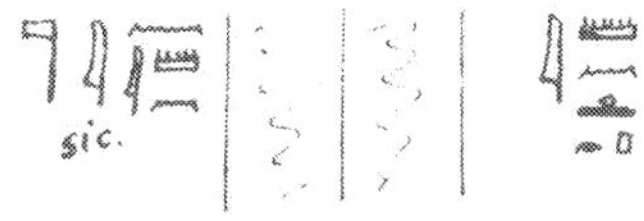

Text 12

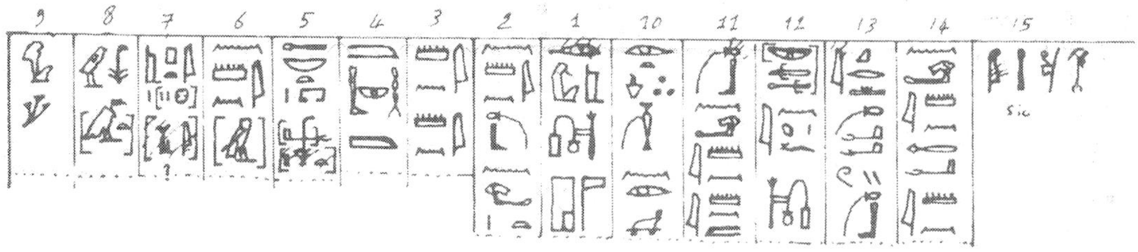

Text 13

1a

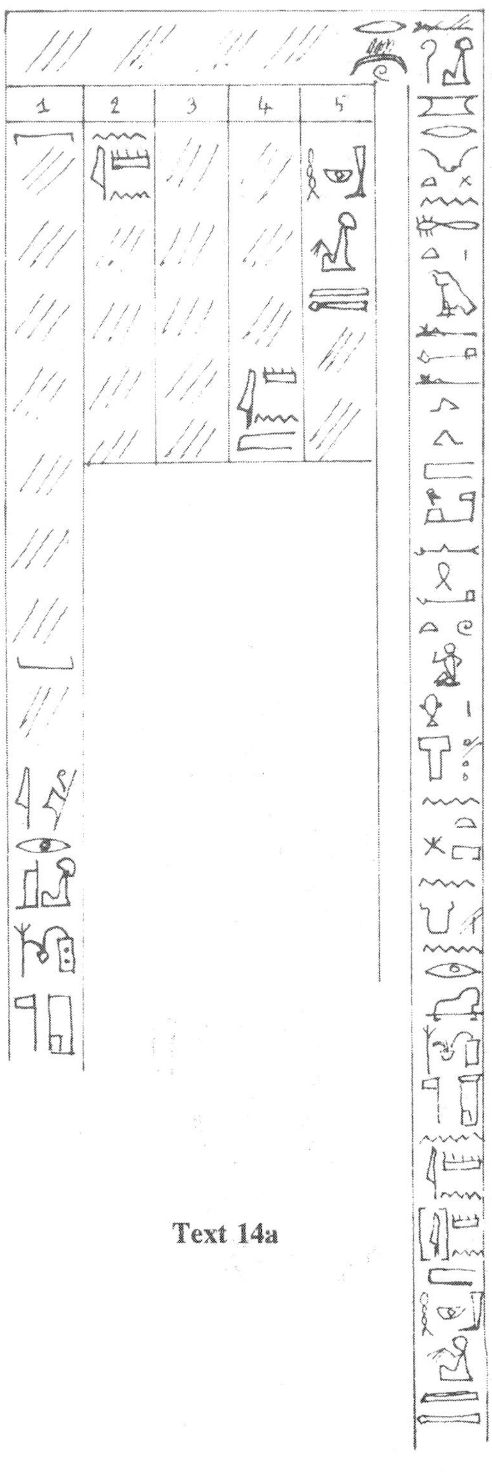

Text 14a

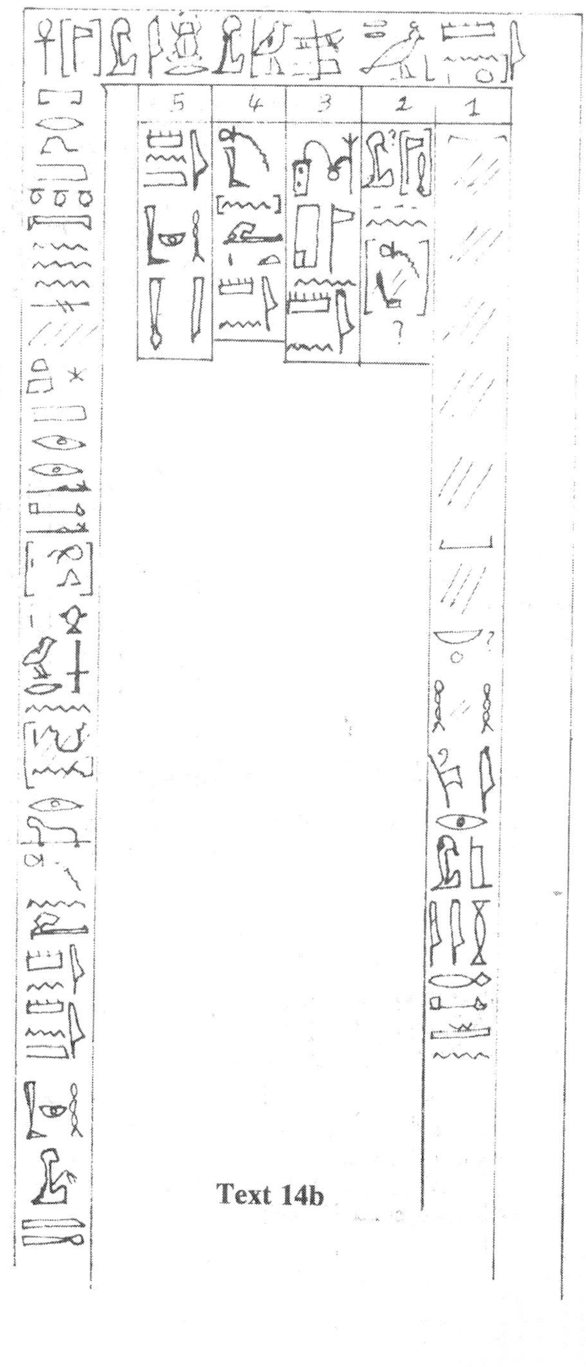

1a

Text 14b

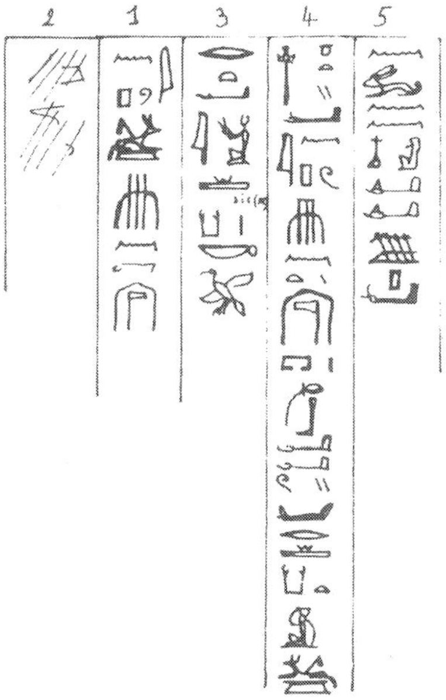

Text 15b

Text 15a

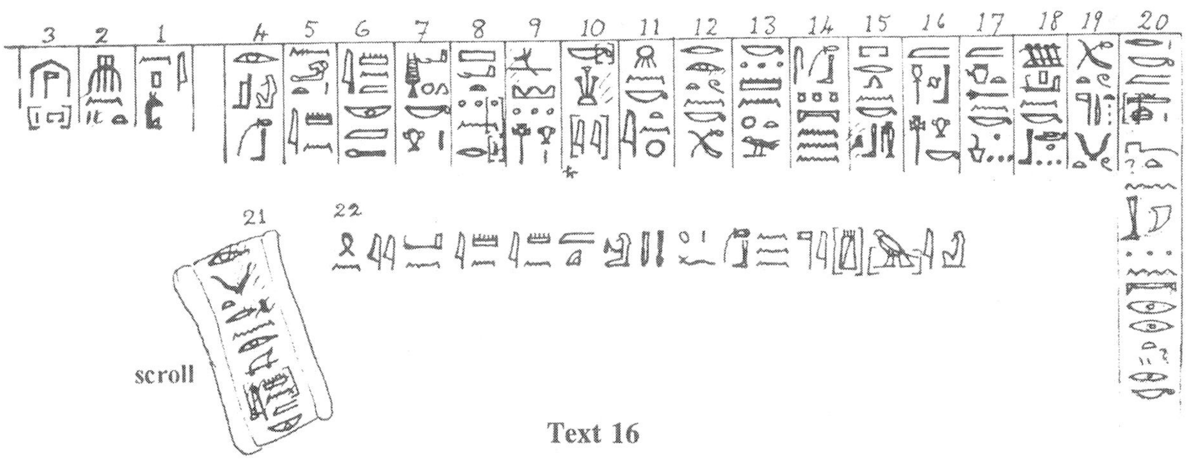

Text 16

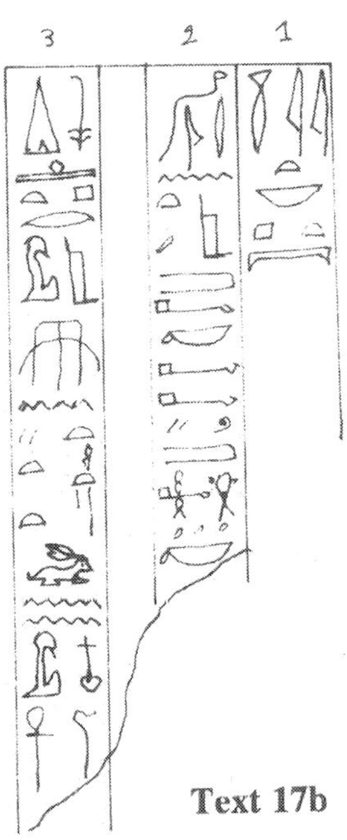

Text 17b

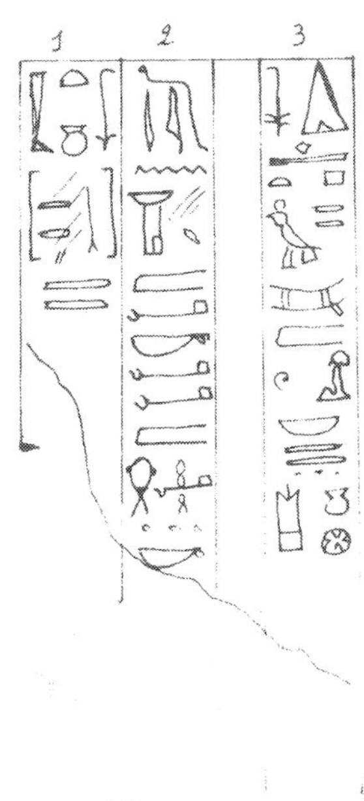

Text 17a

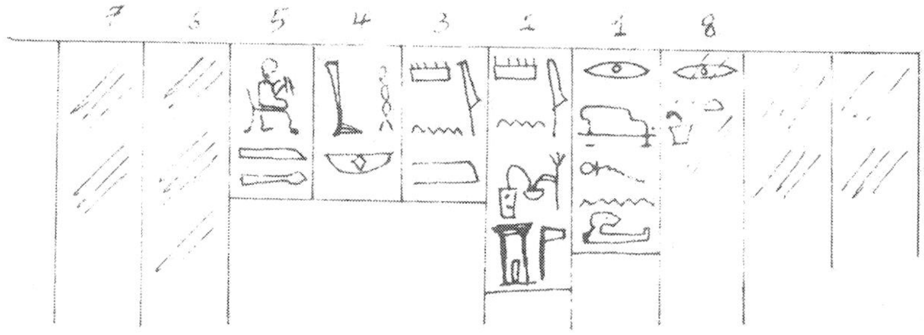

**Text 18**

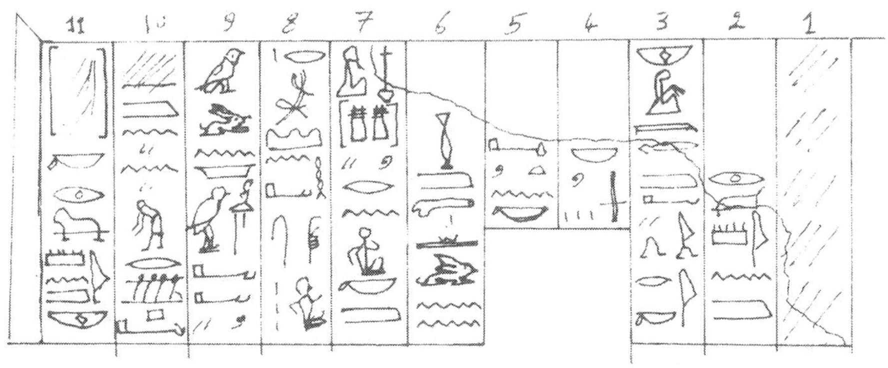

**Text 19**

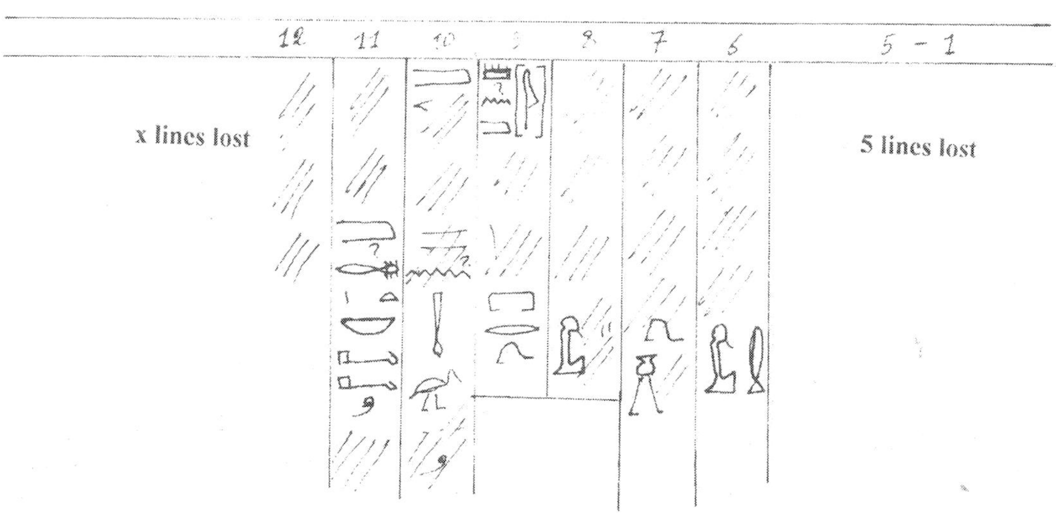


**Text 20**

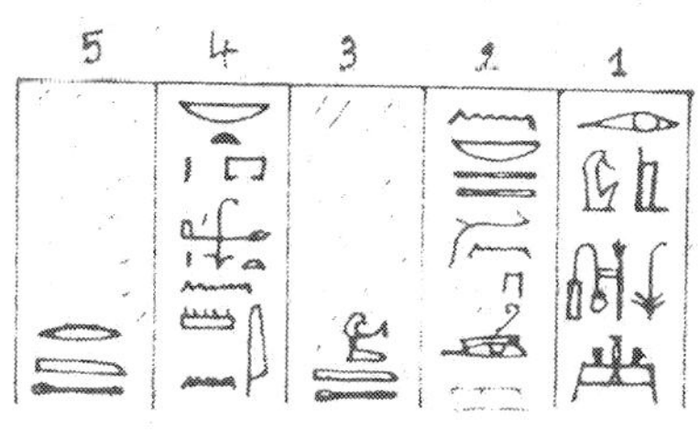

**Text 21**

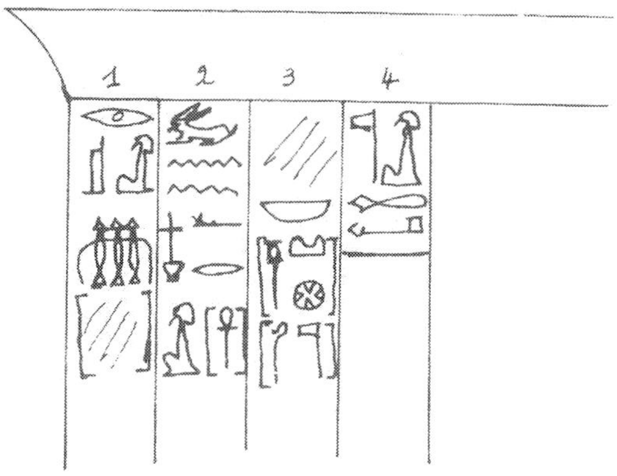


**Text 22**

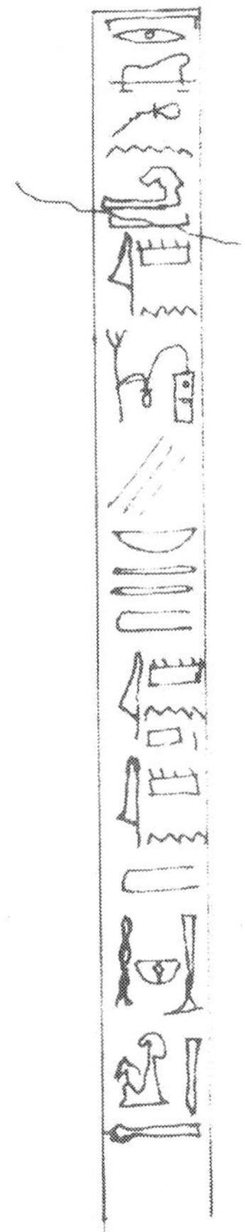

**Text 23**

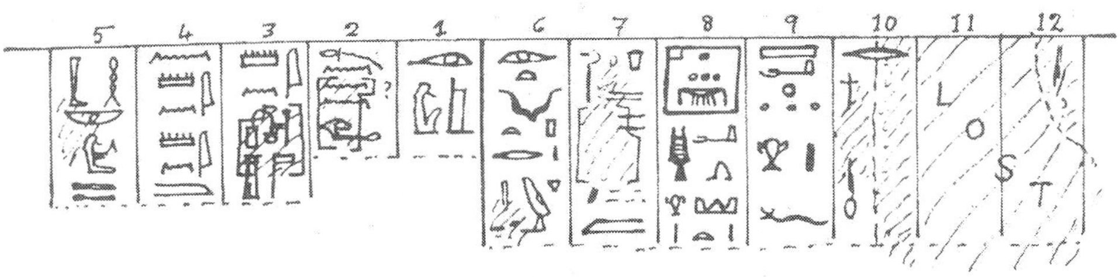


**Text 24**

**Text 25a**

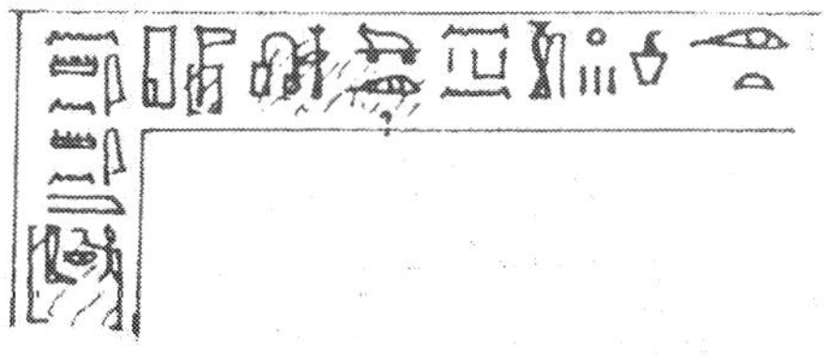

**Text 25b**

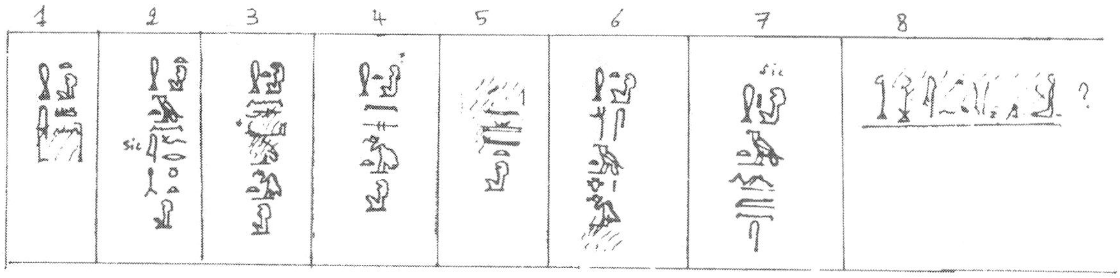

**Text 26**

**Text 27**

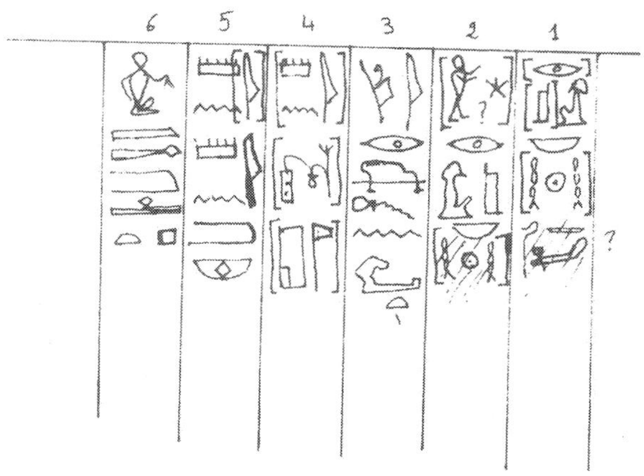

**Text 28**

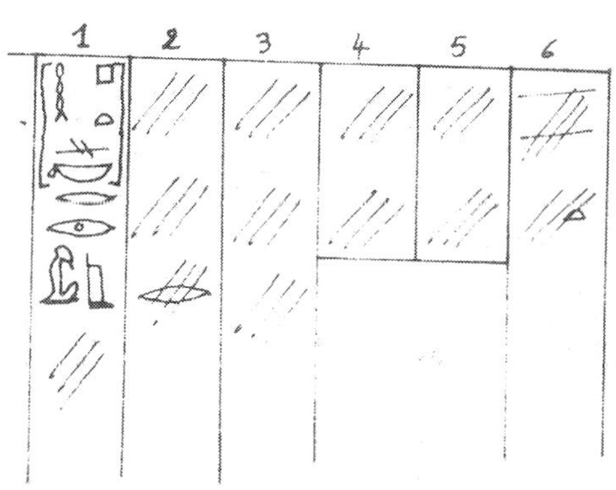

**Text 29**

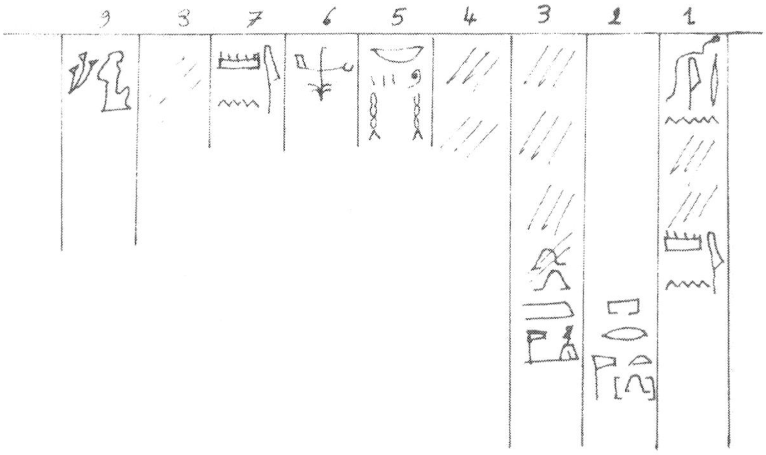

**Text 30**

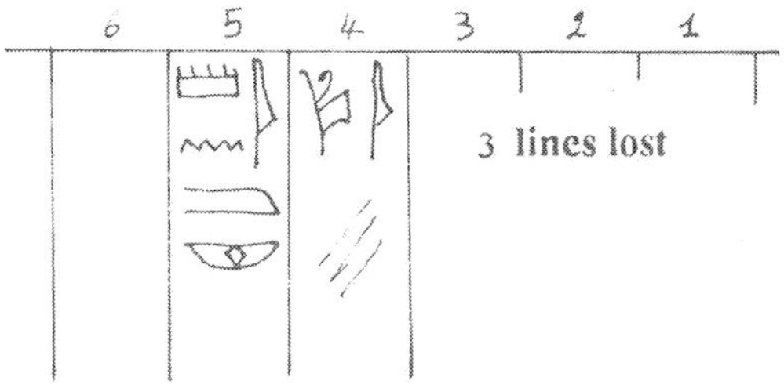


**Text 31**

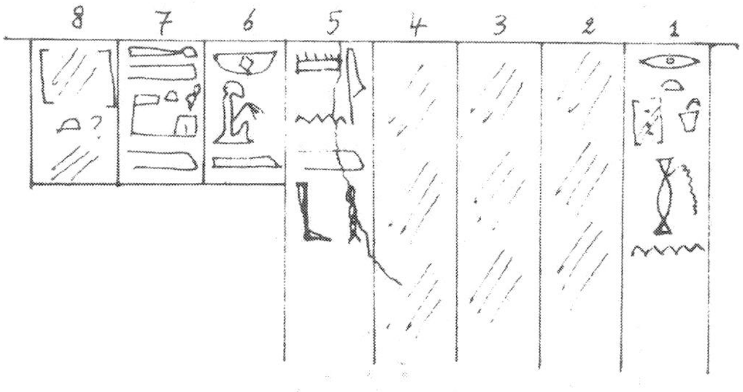

**Text 32**

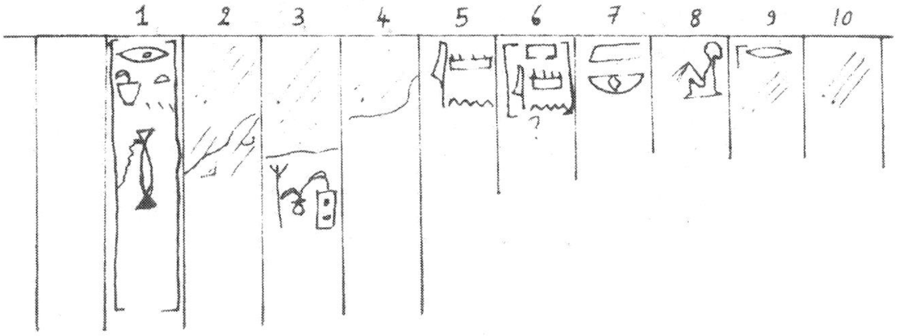

**Text 33**

PLATE A

A1 Entry to T. 44

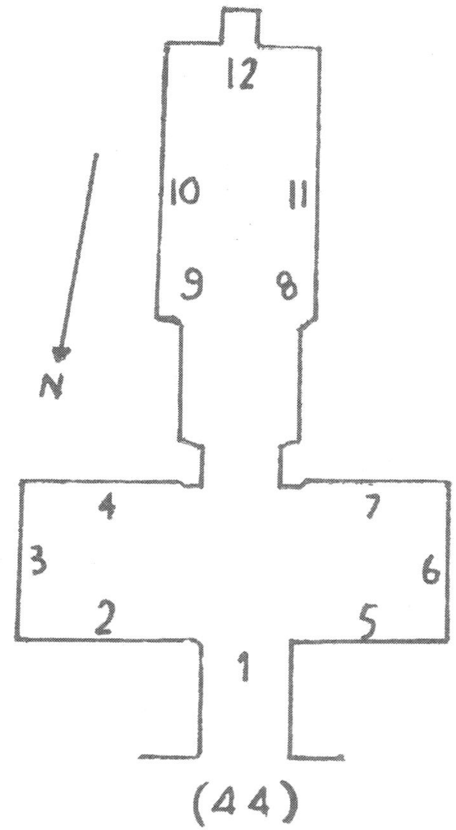


A2 Plan after *PM*

PLATE B

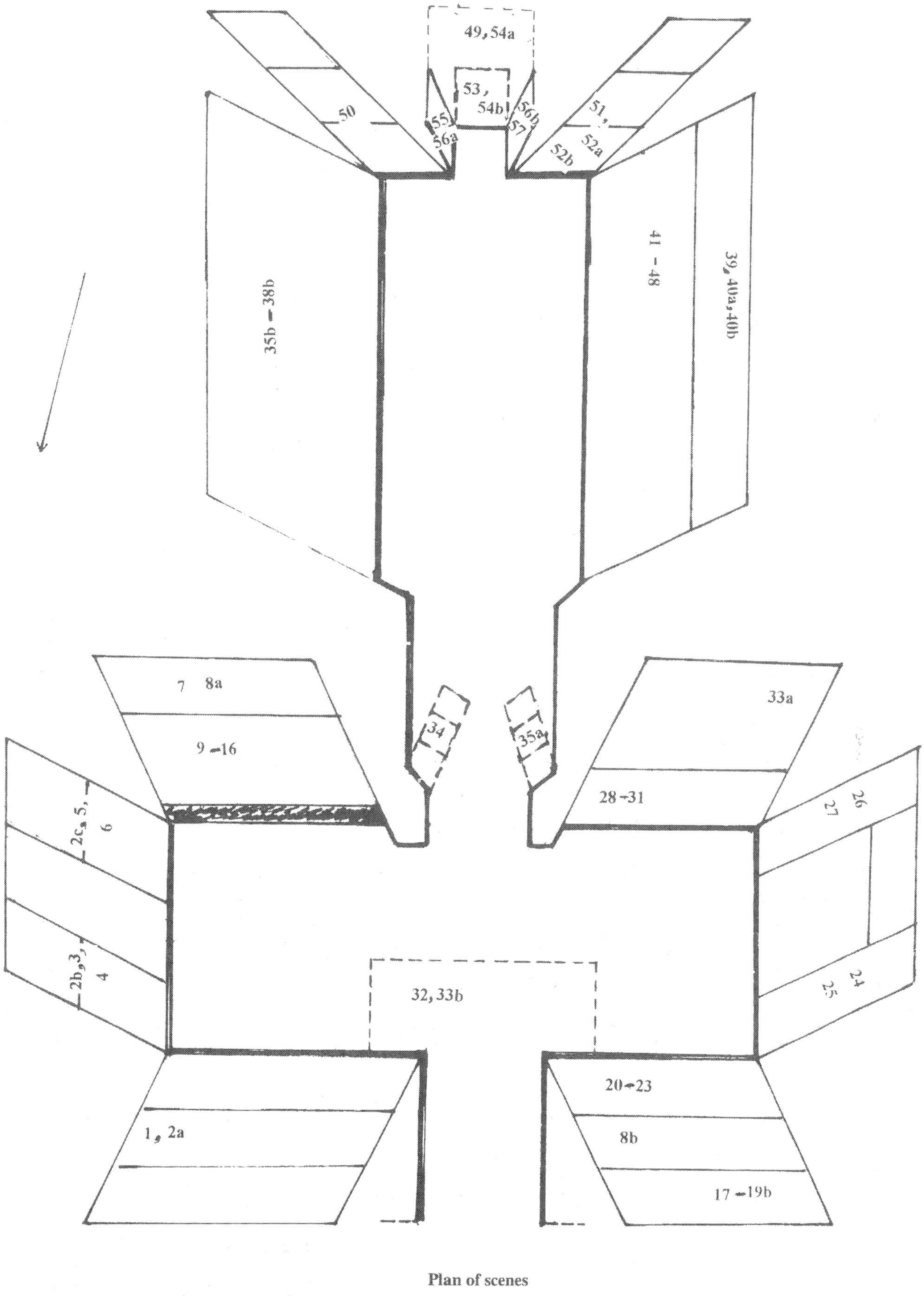


Plan of scenes

PLATE 1

B H Left half : N Wall, middle register

2a B H Left half : N Wall, middle register

2b B H Left half : E Wall, left side

2c B H Left half : E Wall, right side

PLATE 3

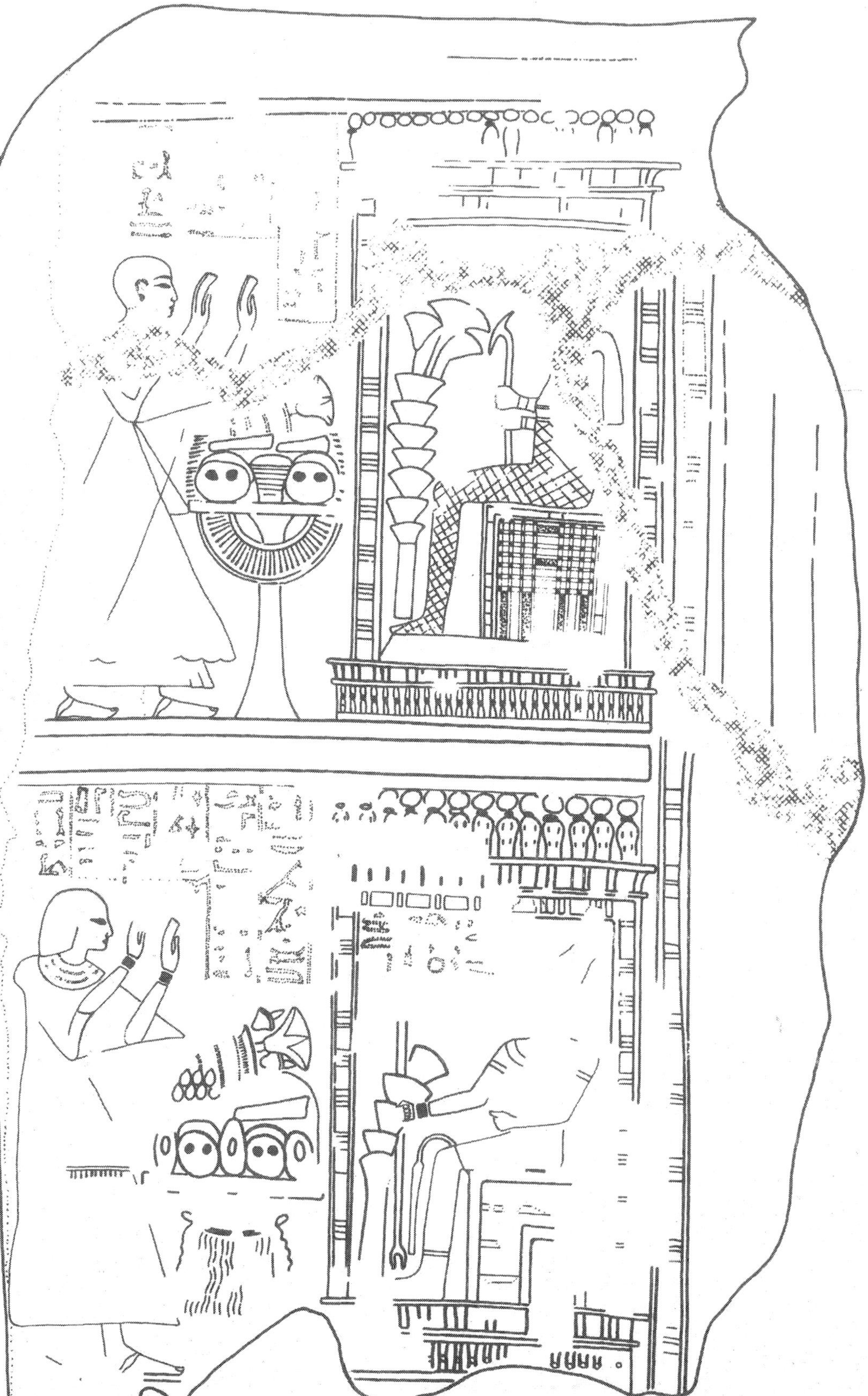

B H  Left half : E Wall, left side

B H Left half : E Wall, left side

B H Left half : E Wall, right side

PLATE 6

B H Left half : S Wall, upper register

PLATE 7

B H Left half : S Wall, upper register

8a B H Left half : S Wall, upper register

8b B H Left half : N Wall, middle register

B H  Left half : S Wall, lower register

B H Left half : S Wall, lower register

PLATE 11

B H Left half : S Wall, lower register

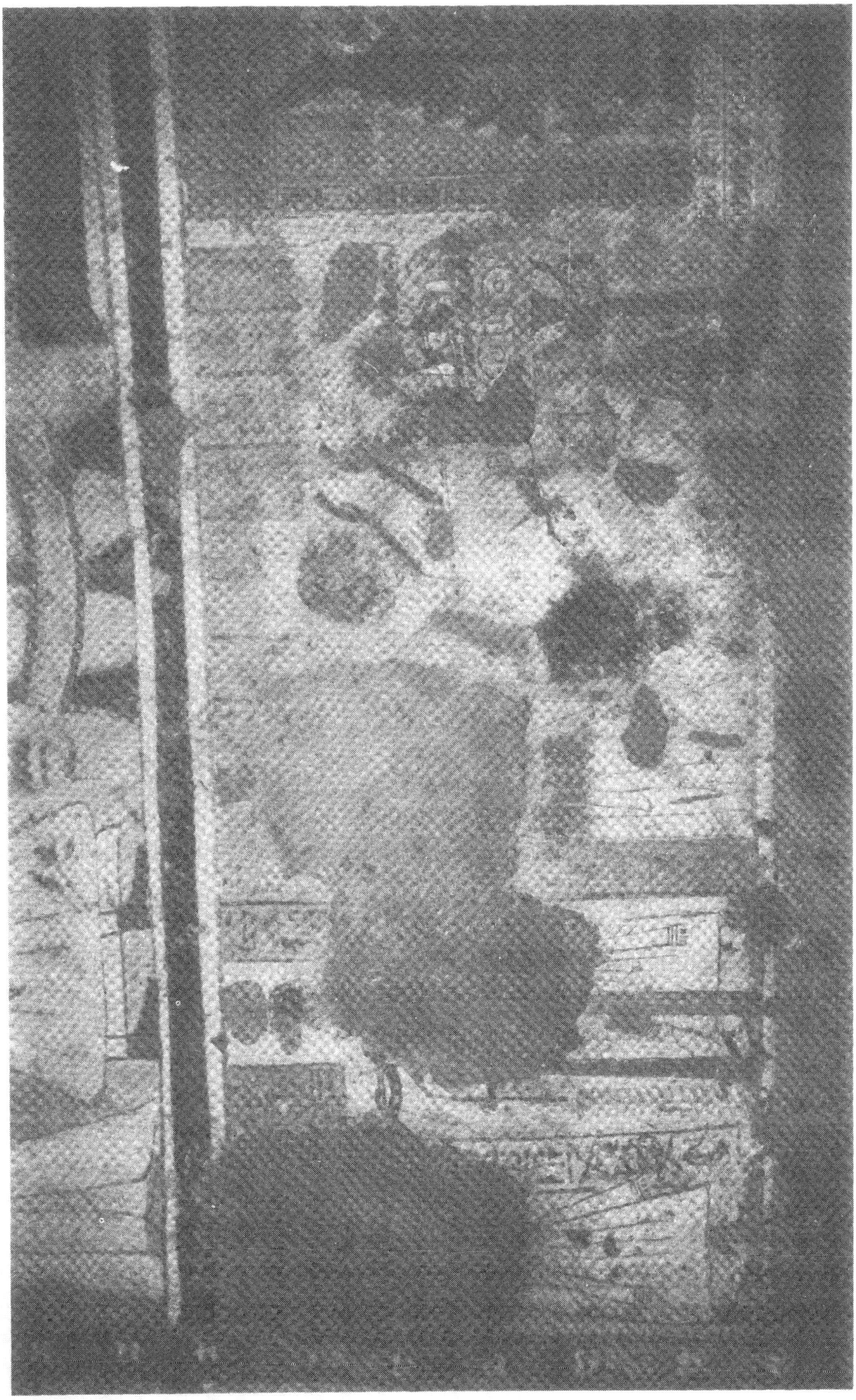

B H Left half : S Wall, lower register

PLATE 13

B H Left half : S Wall, lower register

B H Left half : S Wall, lower register

PLATE 15

B H Left half : S Wall, lower register

PLATE 16

B H Left half : S Wall, lower register

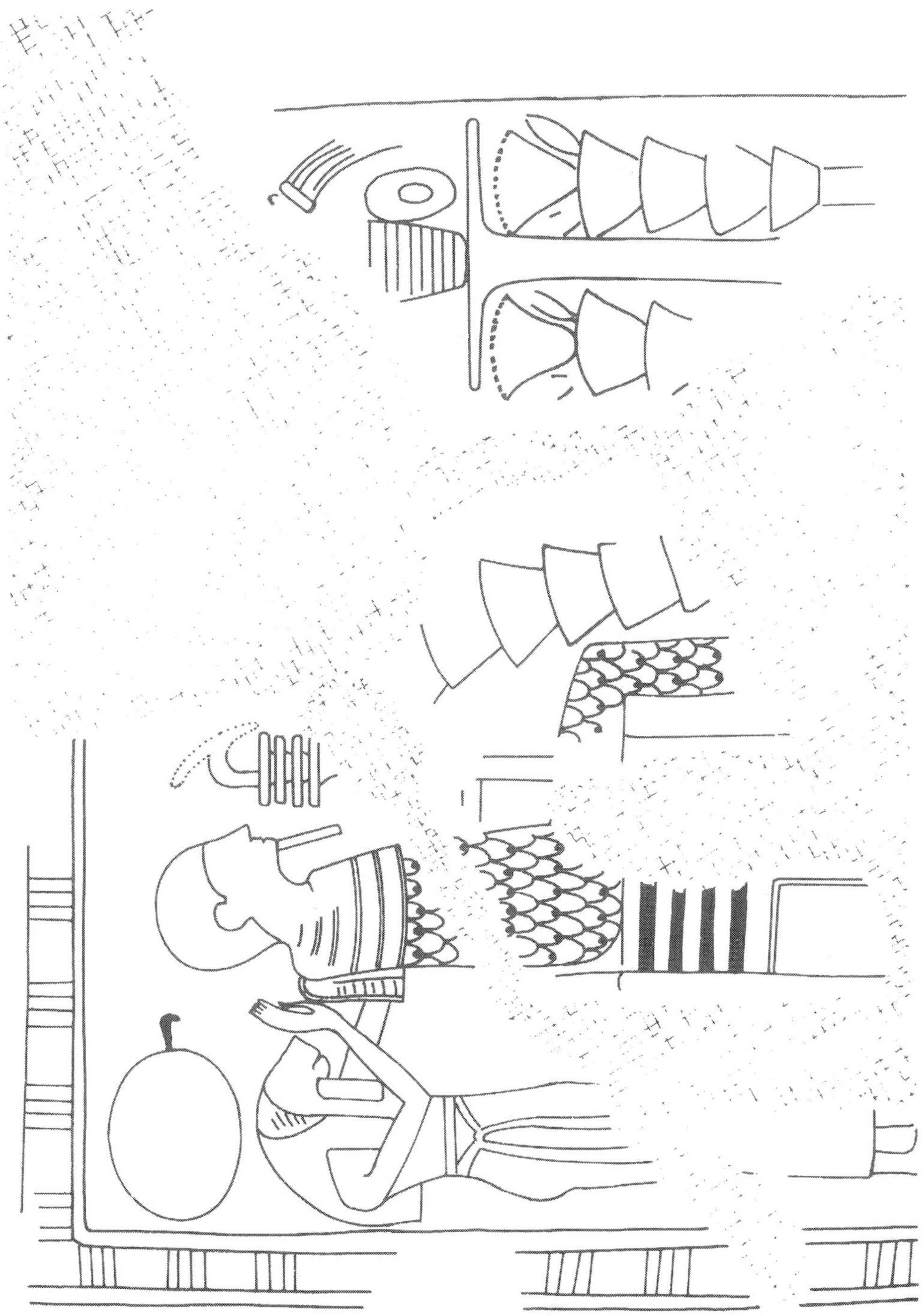

B H Right half : N Wall, upper register

PLATE 18

B H Right half : N Wall, upper register

19a B H Right half : N Wall, upper register

19b B H Right half : N Wall, upper register

PLATE 20

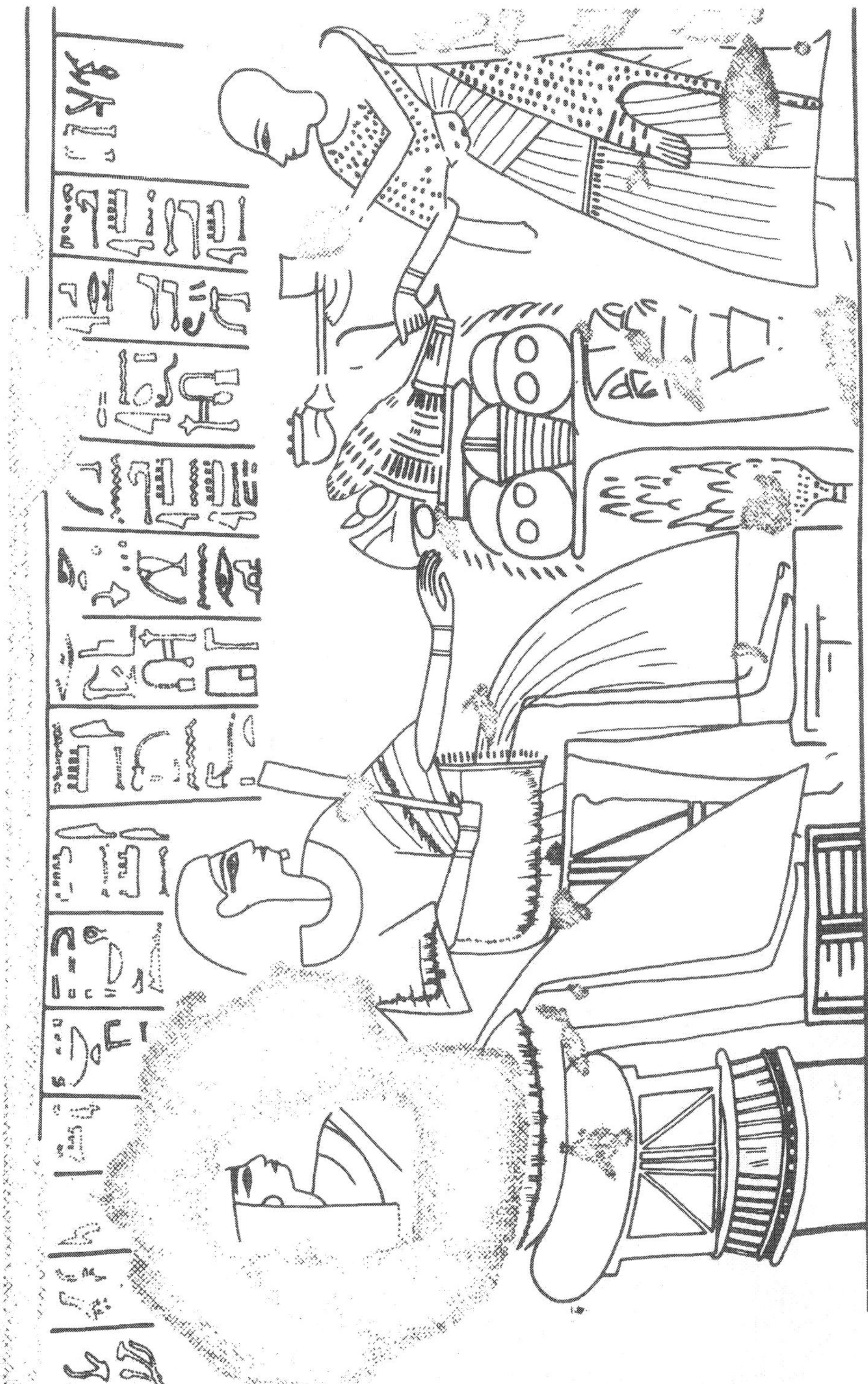

B H Right half : N Wall, lower register

B H Right half : N Wall, lower register

# PLATE 22

B H Right half : N Wall, lower register

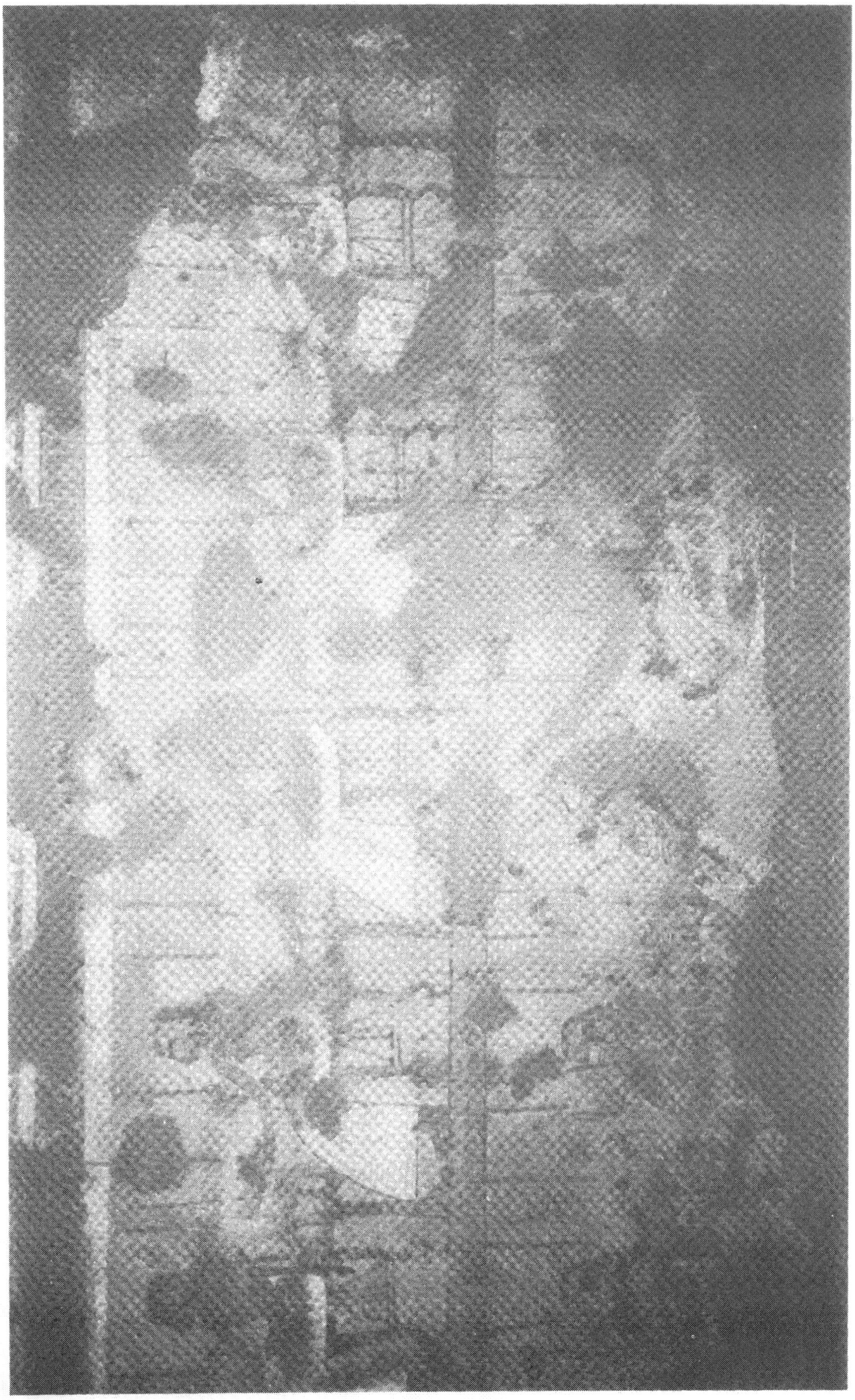

B H Right half : N Wall, lower register

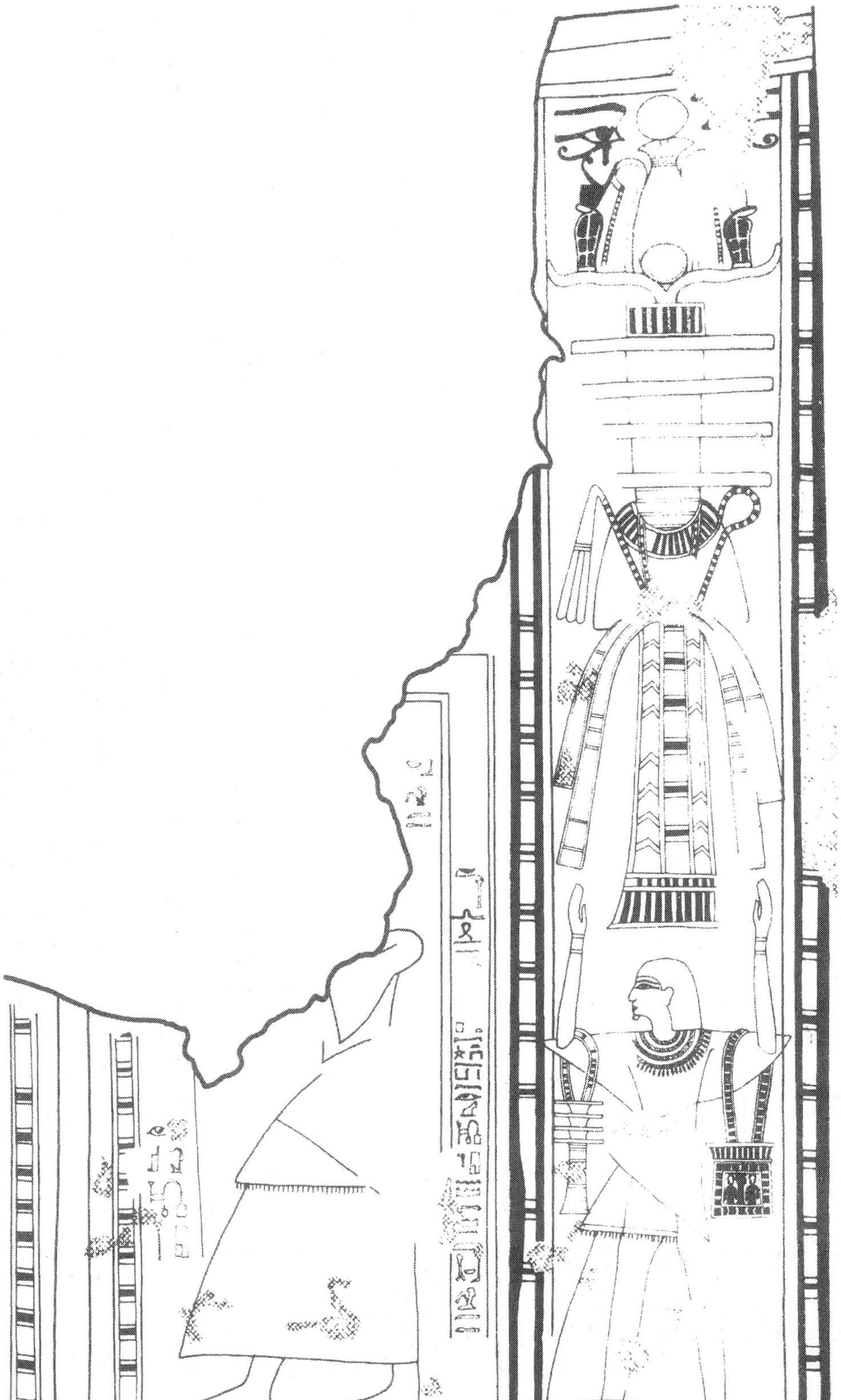

B H Right half : W Wall, right side

B H Right half : W Wall, right side

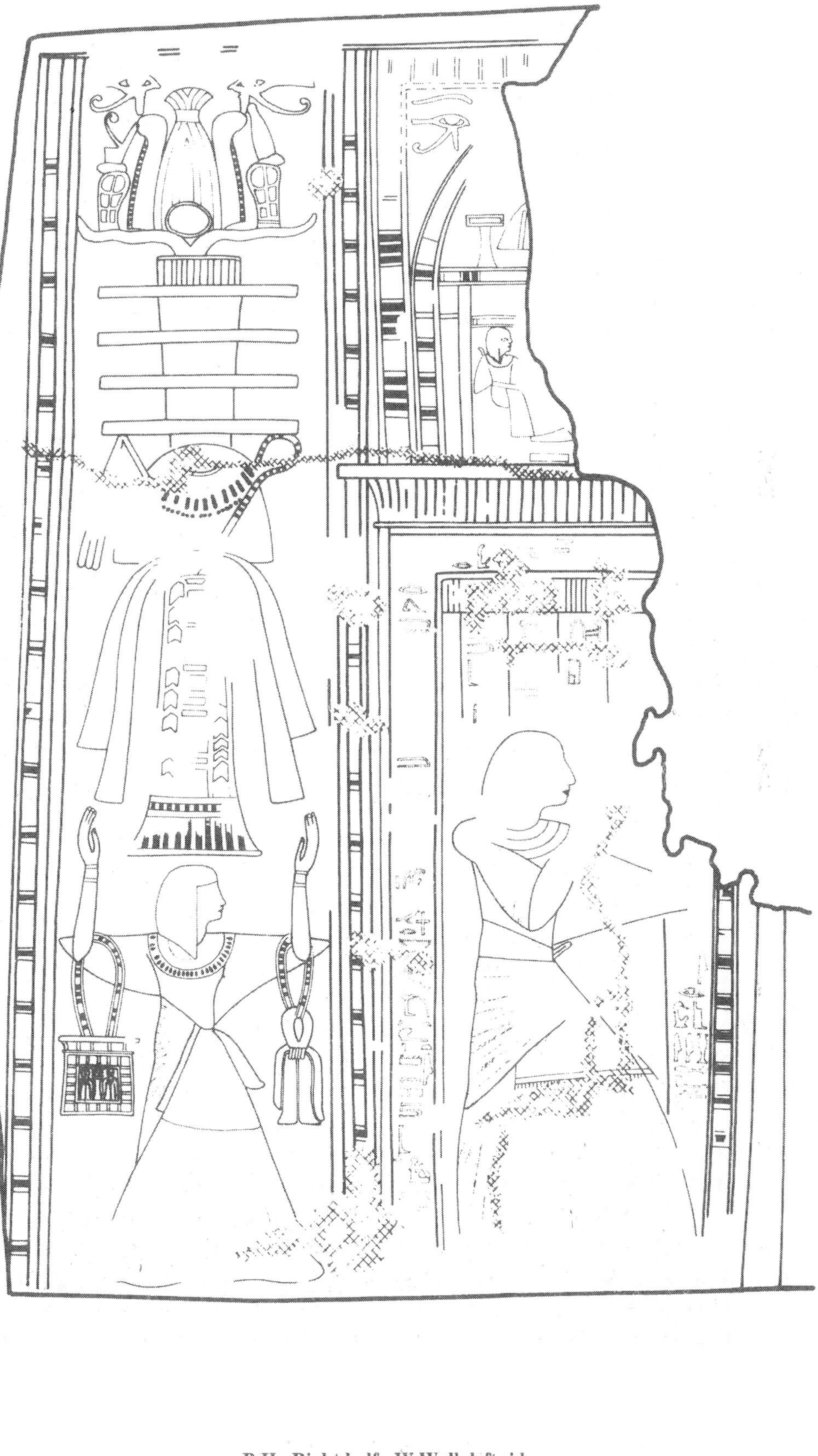

B H Right half : W Wall, left side

B H Right half : W Wall, left side

PLATE 28

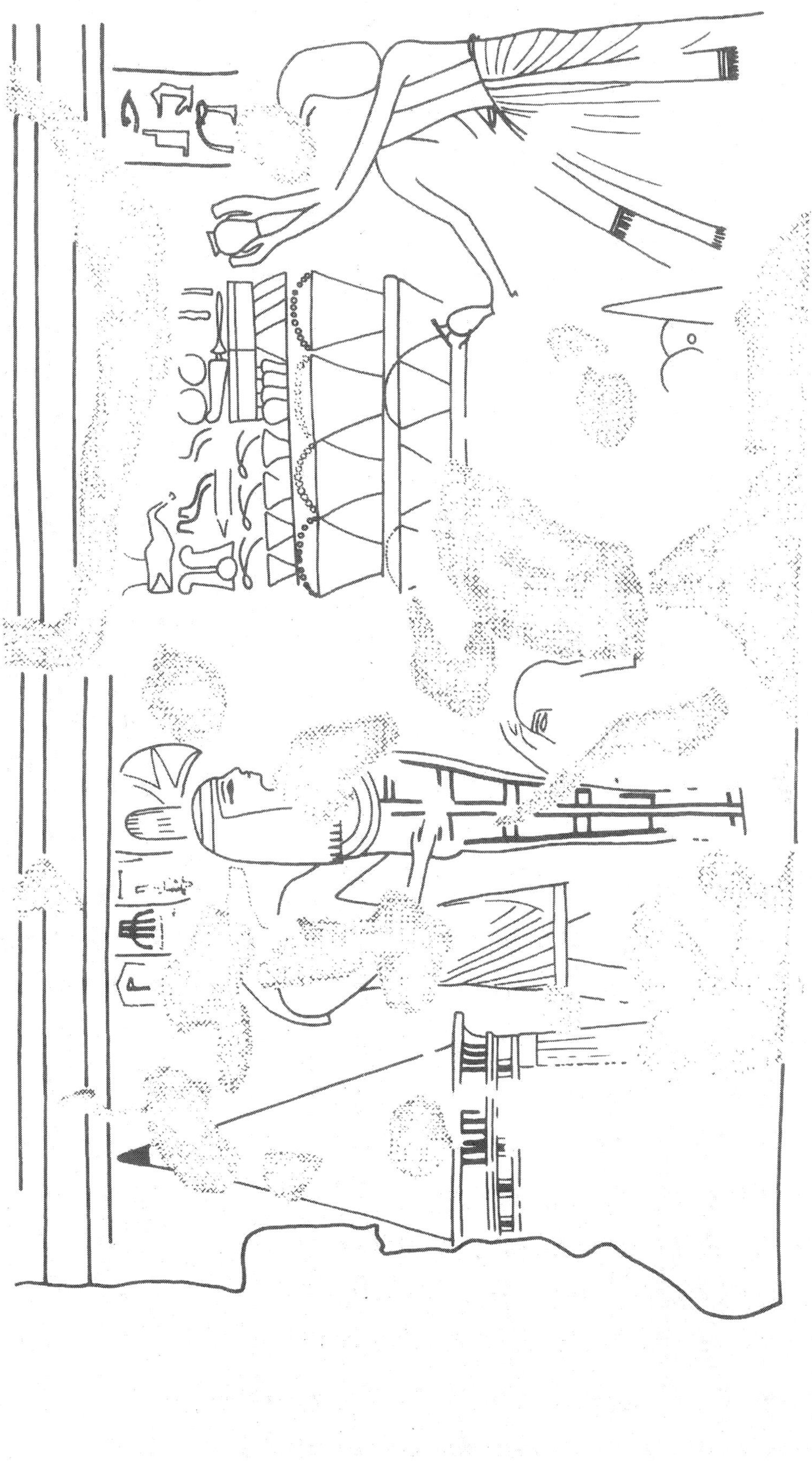

B H Right half : S Wall, lower register

PLATE 29

B H Right half : S Wall, lower register

PLATE 30

B H Right half : S Wall, lower register

B H Right half : S Wall, lower register

PLATE 32

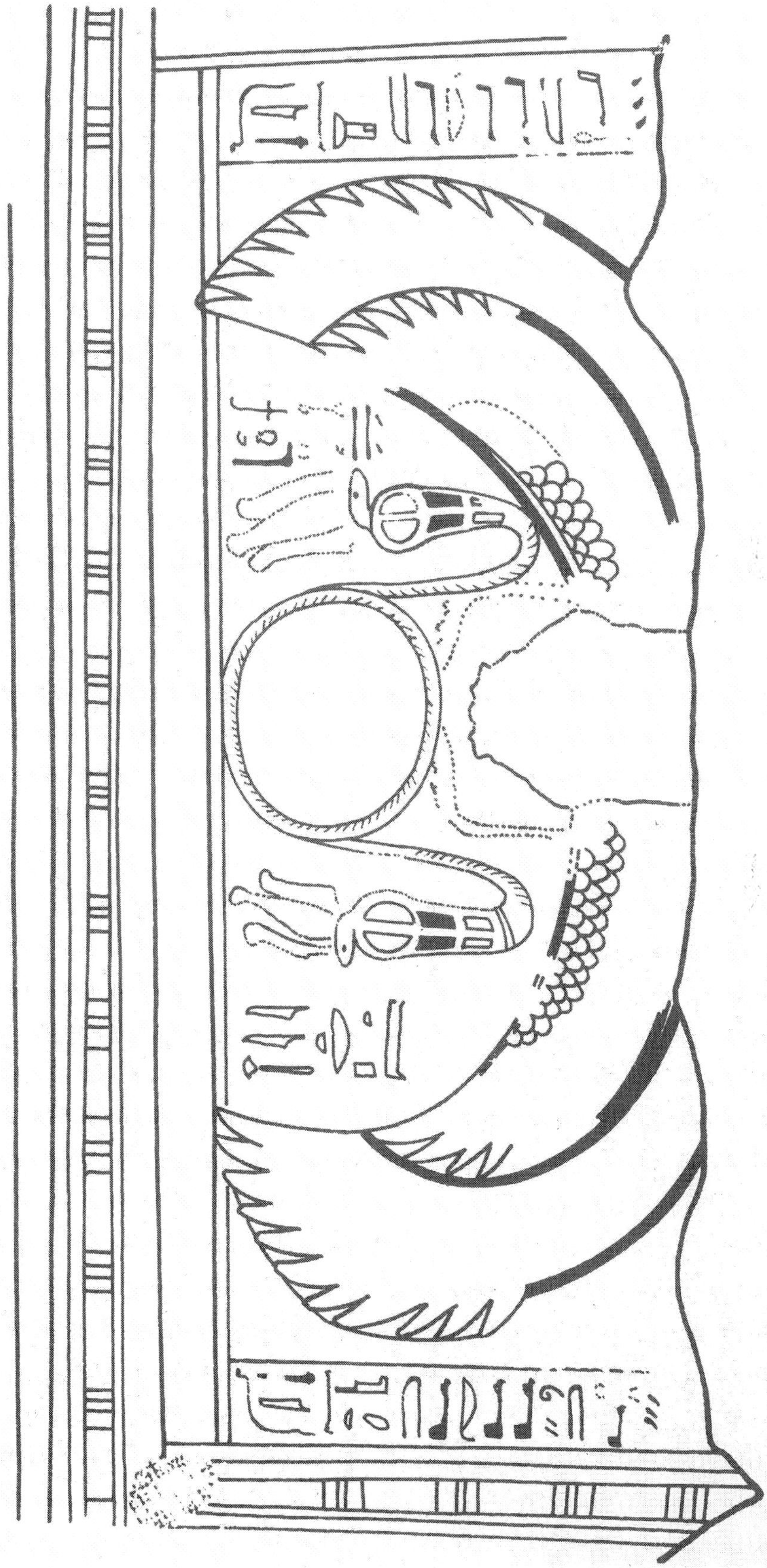

B H The Ceiling

33a B H Right half : S Wall, upper register

33b B H The Ceiling

L H N Wall, right side

35a L H N Wall, left side

35b L H E Wall

L II E Wall

L H E Wall

38b L H E Wall

38a L H E Wall

PLATE 39

L H W Wall, upper register

40a L H W Wall, upper register

40b L H W Wall, upper register

L H W Wall, lower register

L H W Wall, lower register

PLATE 43

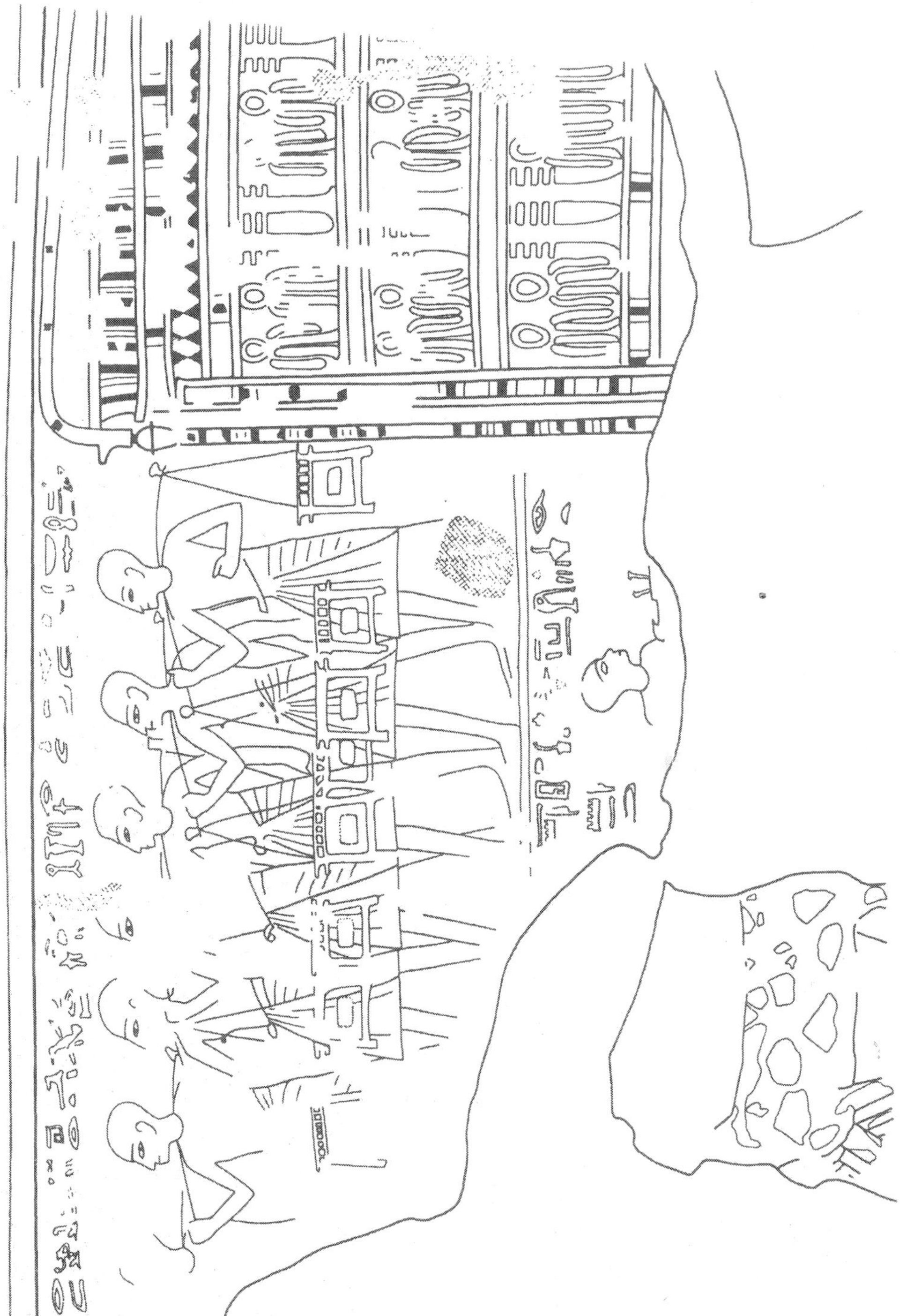

L H W Wall, lower register

PLATE 44

L H W Wall, lower register

PLATE 45

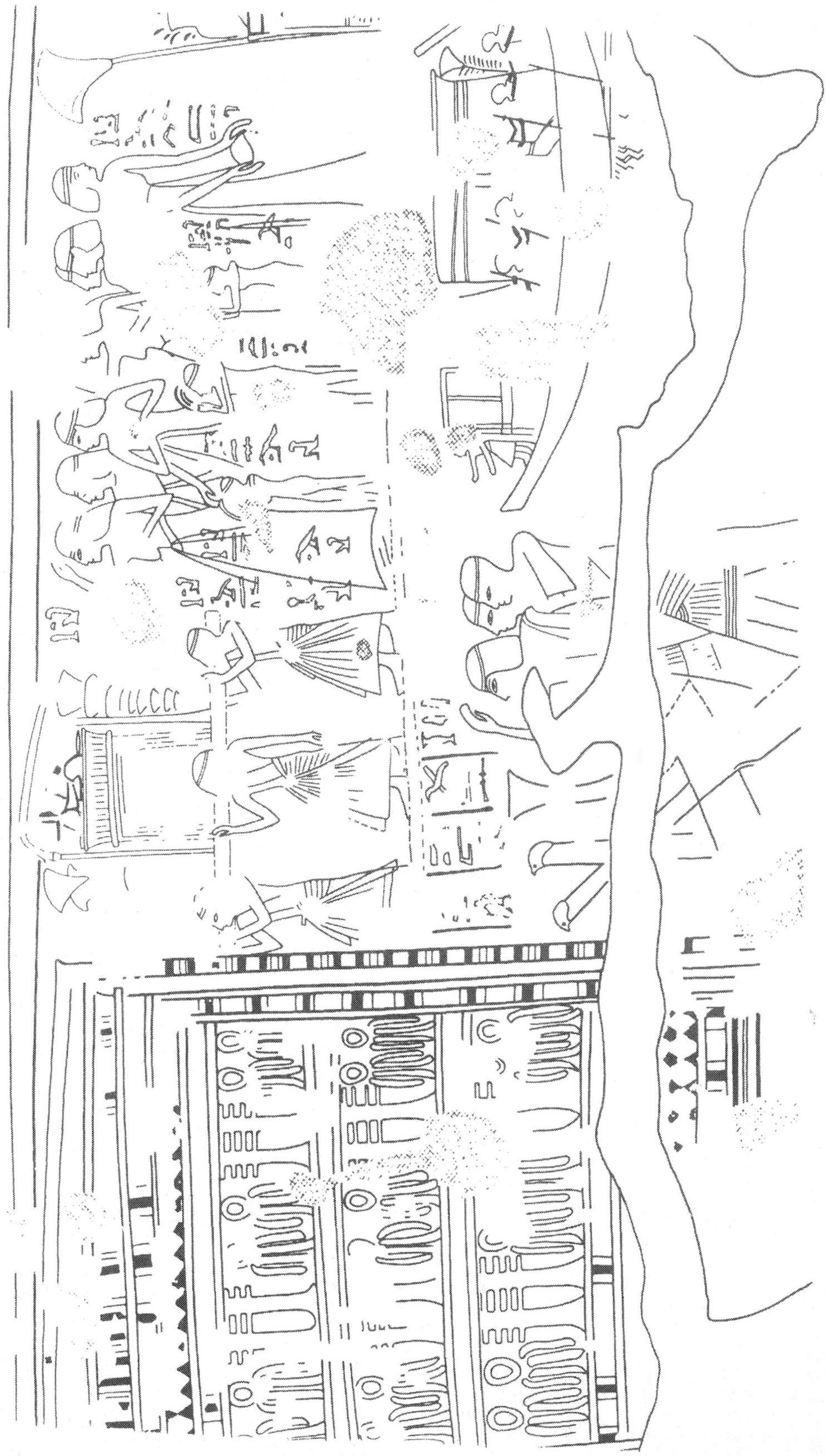

L H W Wall, lower register

L H W Wall, lower register

PLATE 47

L H W Wall, lower register

L H W Wall, lower register

PLATE 49

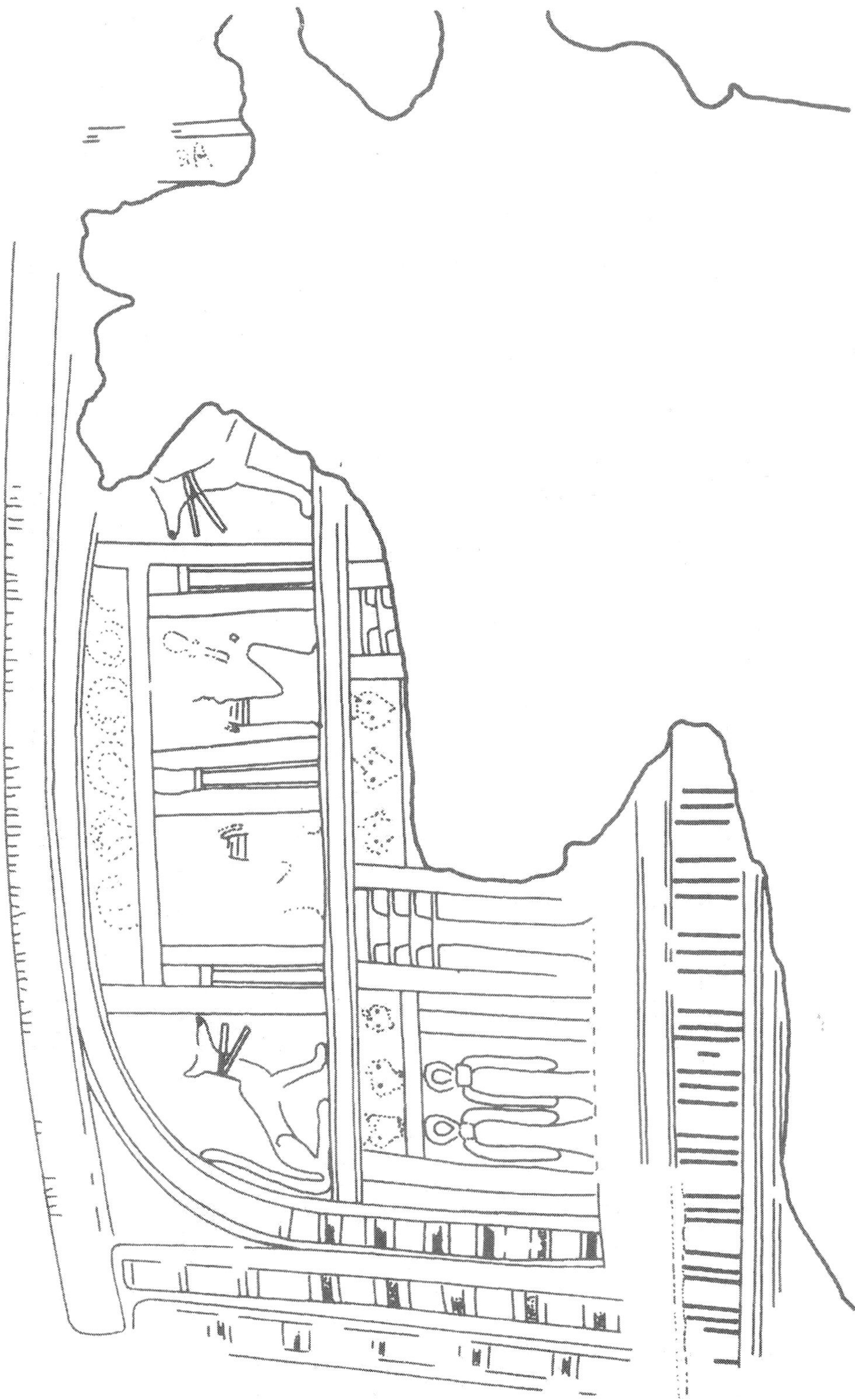

L H S Wall, upper register

L H S Wall, middle & lower register, left side

PLATE 51

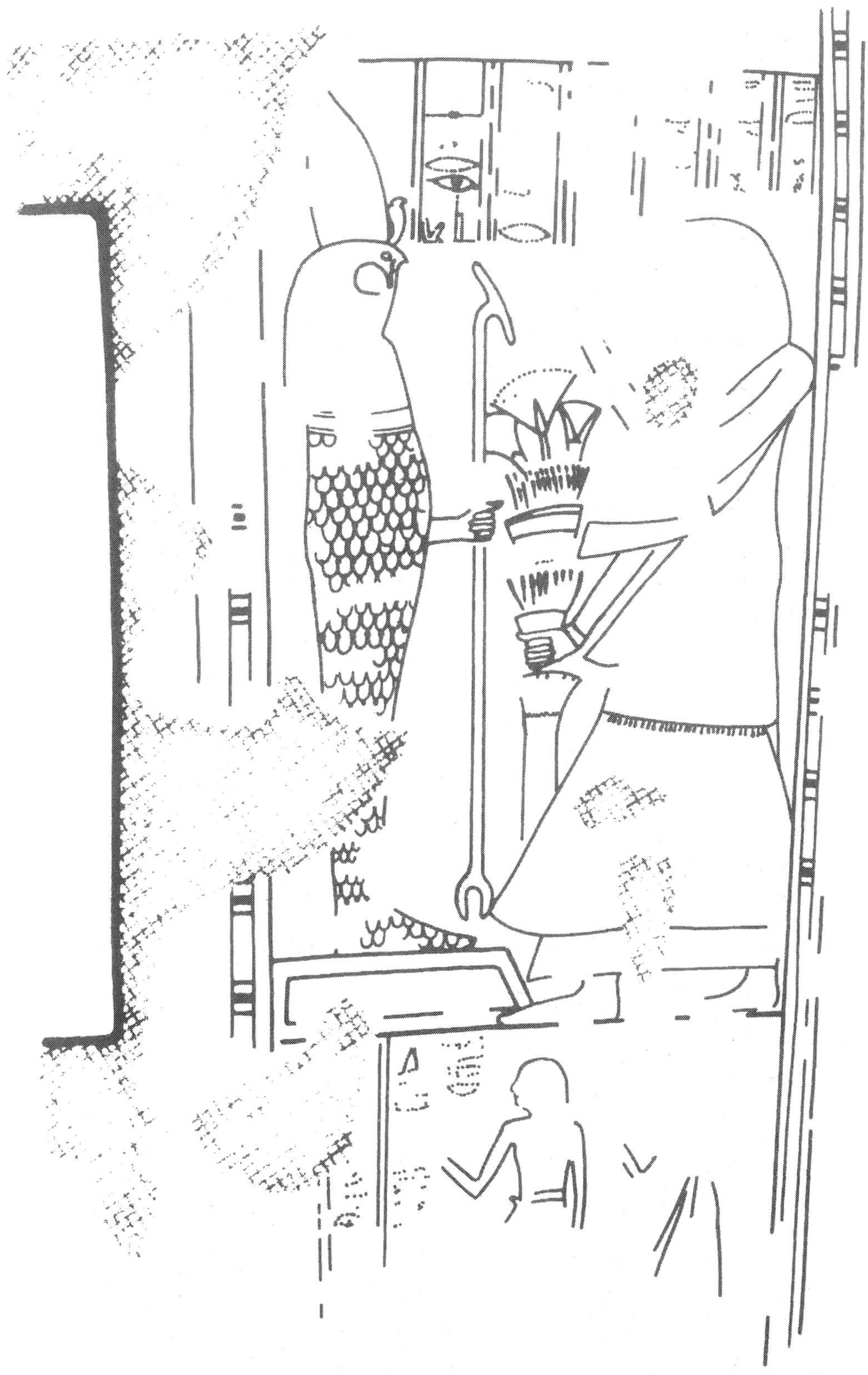

L H S Wall, middle & lower register, right side

52a  L H  S Wall, middle & lower register, right side

52b  L H  S Wall, lower register

L H S Wall, The Niche, rear wall

54a L H S Wall, upper register

54b L H S Wall, The Niche, rear wall

PLATE 55

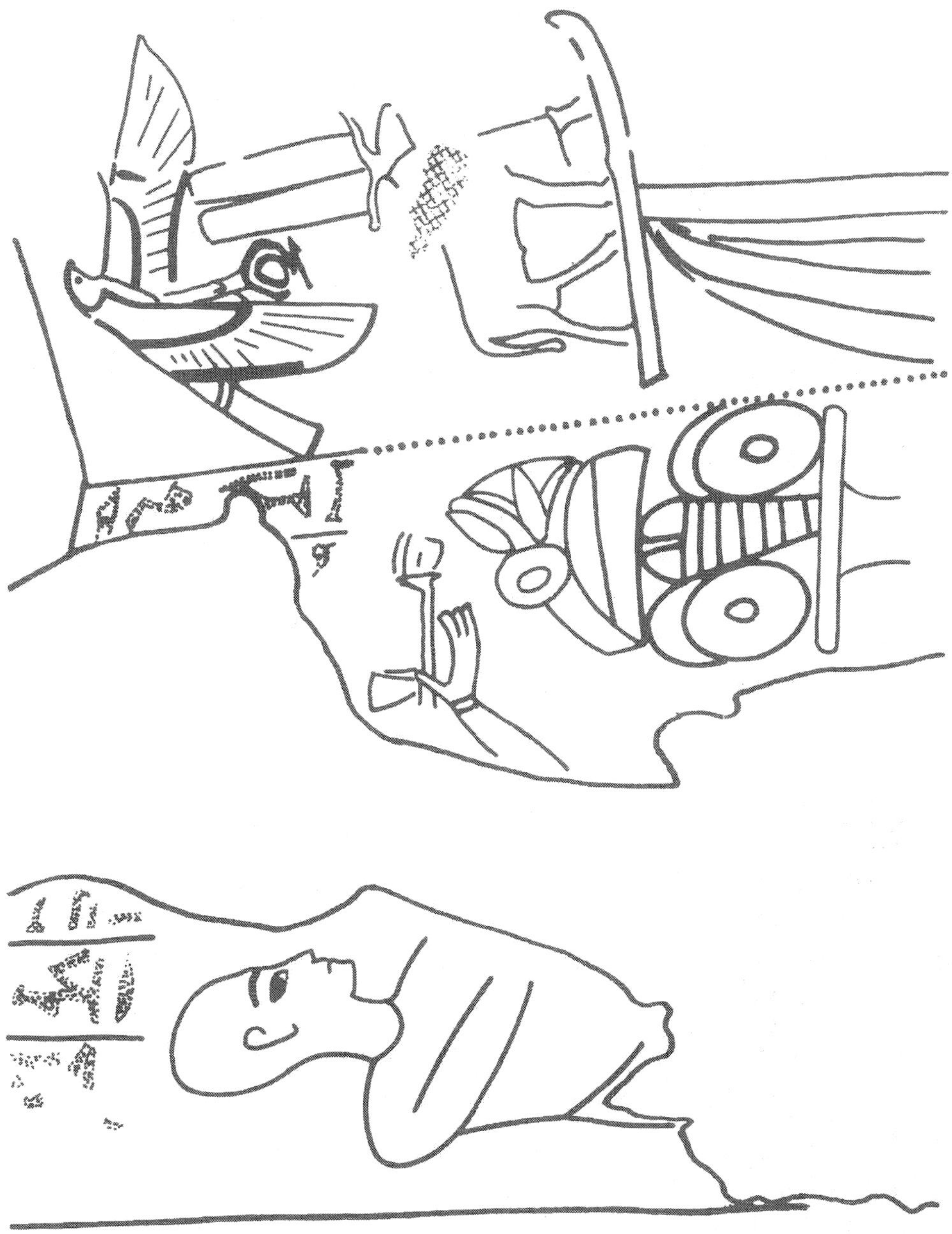

L H S Wall, The Niche, left wall

# PLATE 56

56a L H S Wall, The Niche, left wall

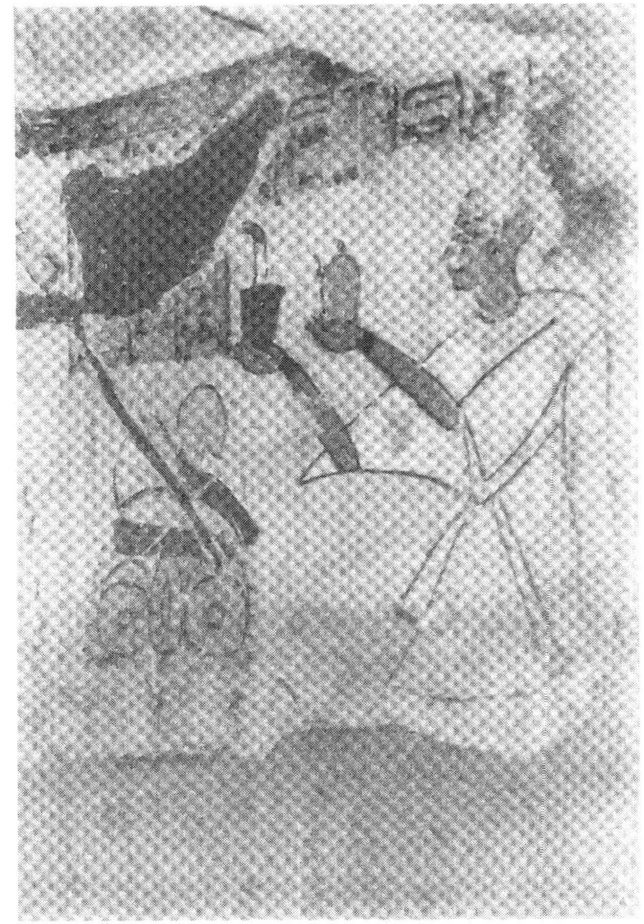

56b L H S Wall, The Niche, right wall

PLATE 57

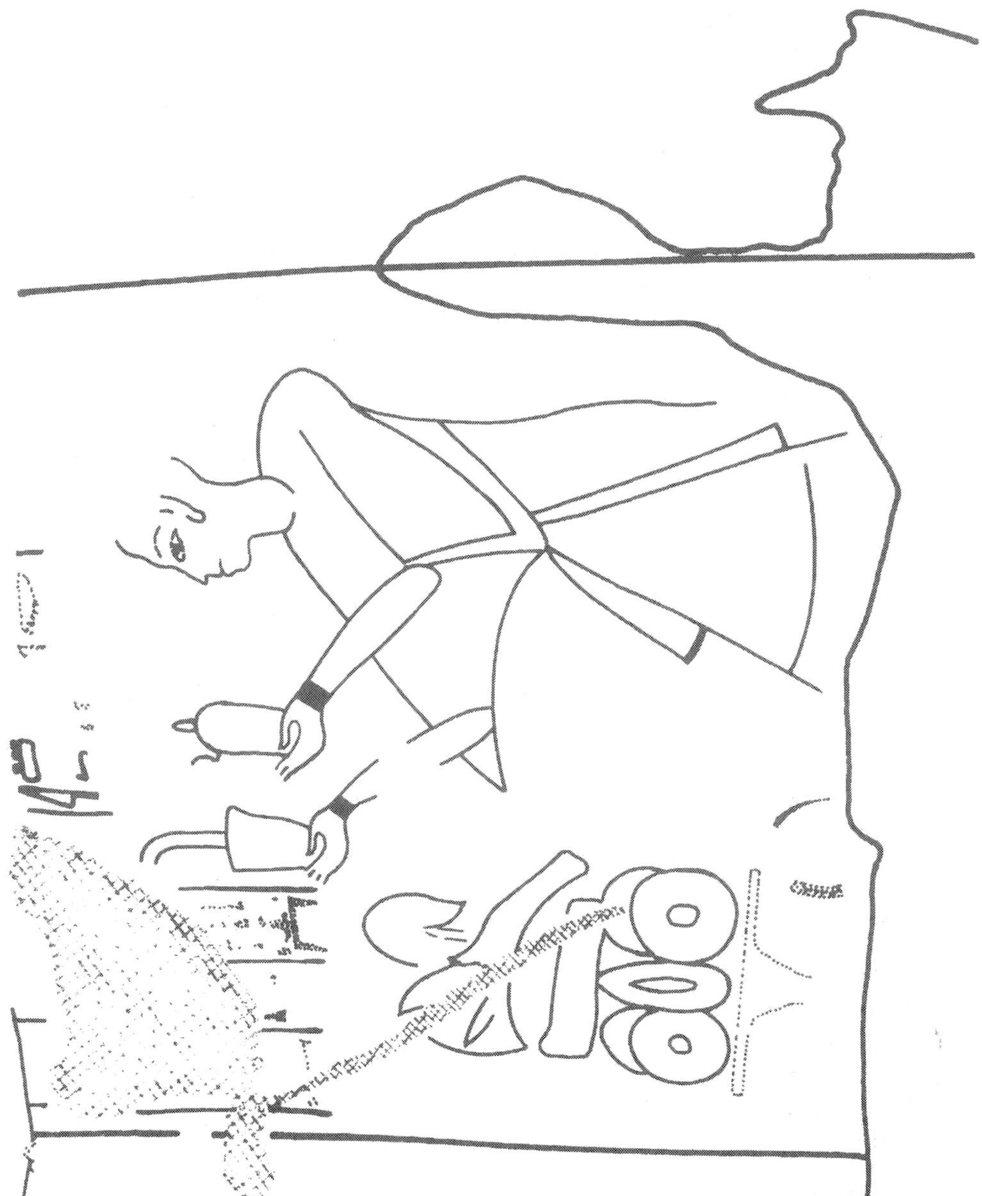

L H S Wall, The Niche, right wall